OECD Public Governance Reviews

Mexico's National Auditing System

STRENGTHENING ACCOUNTABLE GOVERNANCE

OECD

BETTER POLICIES FOR BETTER LIVES

Please cite this publication as:
OECD (2017), *Mexico's National Auditing System: Strengthening Accountable Governance*, OECD Public Governance Reviews, OECD Publishing, Paris.
http://dx.doi.org/10.1787/9789264264748-en

ISBN 978-92-64-26473-1 (print)
ISBN 978-92-64-26474-8 (PDF)

Series: OECD Public Governance Reviews
ISSN 2219-0406 (print)
ISSN 2219-0414 (online)

Photo credits: Cover © shoo_arts/iStock/Thinkstock.

Corrigenda to OECD publications may be found on line at: *www.oecd.org/about/publishing/corrigenda.htm*.

Foreword

Recent reforms in Mexico have established a new legal architecture for strengthening public governance and upholding the principles of accountability, integrity and transparency in government. The National Auditing System (Sistema Nacional de Fiscalización, or SNF) is a critical pillar in this architecture.

The OECD's whole-of-government approach recognises that creating better policies for better lives relies on the contributions of many drivers of change. Supreme audit institutions (SAIs) represent one critical driver in a system of governance actors, and their role is evolving. Many SAIs are going beyond their traditional oversight role to being purveyors of evidence and analysis in support of a richer policy dialogue.

Mexico's approach to recent reforms aligns with the OECD's whole-of-government perspective, which emphasises the need for co-ordination and coherence across policy areas, branches and levels of government. The SNF itself exemplifies this approach. It brings together national and sub-national accountability actors, providing a platform for co-ordination, information sharing and for driving tangible improvements in governance.

With secondary legislation for strengthening accountability, integrity and transparency approved in July 2016, committed action from government and other stakeholders will be essential for effectively implementing reforms and delivering results to citizens. In support of this next step, the OECD partnered with Mexico's supreme audit institution, the Auditoria Superior de la Federación (ASF).

Changes in legislation expand ASF's mandate and powers, and establish the legal foundation for it to improve its impact and relevance. For instance, ASF will now report to the Mexican Congress twice more throughout the fiscal year on the state of public expenditures, and it will take on a new investigative role to curb administrative irregularities. However, greater authority and responsibilities comes with challenges and risks.

This report offers insights on strategic actions and activities that ASF can take to leverage its comparative advantage in auditing in order to enhance its contributions to accountable governance and avoid overextension. To this end, ASF could take a number of actions, such as adapting its risk-based audit programming to more strategically allocate its resources and better serve Congress. It could also complement its investigations with additional reviews that offer solutions to systemic problems in government that undermine integrity.

This report also explores approaches for the SNF, as well as sub-national audit institutions, to fulfil their roles in a system of accountability actors. For instance, legal, policy and implementation gaps threaten the independence, capacity and coherence of auditing at the state level. The SNF could address these gaps in a number of ways, including harmonisation of standards for internal control and risk management, as well as improving the professional audit service in states and municipalities.

Going beyond audit institutions, a systems-based approach to accountable governance relies on the commitment of many actors, including Congress. This report also shows the potential for Congress to make greater use of ASF's audit reports and improve its own technical capacity, thereby reinforcing the accountability chain.

The OECD's work draws insights from numerous methodologies and sources of information, including interviews, literature reviews, comparative benchmarking studies, policy expertise and the experiences of three Mexican states (Coahuila, Puebla, and Querétaro). OECD experts across a range of governance issues, including budgeting, internal control and multi-level governance, helped shape the proposals for action to support the SNF. Experts from peer review countries (Brazil, Germany, Netherlands, United States) also helped to frame analyses and deepen insights based on international experiences.

As Mexico moves from legislating to implementing, accountability actors are at the crux of delivering on the promise of recent reforms. In particular, ASF and other audit institutions operate at the intersection of accountability, integrity and good governance. From this unique position, they offer oversight, insight and foresight for more accountable governance, evidence-based policies, and ultimately, better lives for the people of Mexico.

Angel Gurría
OECD Secretary-General

Acknowledgements

This report was prepared by the Public Sector Integrity Division of the OECD Directorate for Public Governance and Territorial Development. The work was led by Gavin Ugale with major contributions from Natalia Nolan Flecha, Angelos Binis and Jacobo Pastor García Villarreal. Janos Bertok and Julio Bacio Terracino provided valuable guidance and supervision. Alison McMeekin, Guilio Nessi, Chad Burbank and William Begley made important contributions. In addition, Thibaut Gigou managed communications and editing, Julie Harris assisted with copy-editing, and Anaisa Goncalves and Alpha Zambou provided key administrative support.

The authors would like to thank the experts within OECD and the international audit community who supported this effort. This report benefited from the insights and review of a strong team of public policy experts in the Directorate for Public Governance and Territorial Development, including from the Budgeting and Public Expenditures Division. In addition, OECD is grateful for the support, insights and reviews of representatives from various audit institutions from selected OECD and partner countries, including Marcelo André Barboza da Rocha Chaves (Brazil), Ulrich Steinbach (Germany), Ina de Haan (Netherlands) and José Oyola Santiago (United States).

OECD also extends its appreciation to Mexico's Auditoria Superior de la Federación (ASF) for its initiative and openness throughout the process. In particular, the authors would like to thank Auditor General Juan Portal and Benjamín Fuentes, Technical Secretary to the Auditor General, for their leadership, as well as Erwín Alberto Ramirez Gutierrez, Francisco Tomas Parral Pineda, Ileana Rocio Ayala Guzman and Ninoska Martinez for all their support. In addition, OECD appreciates the insights of numerous public officials in the Congress as well as Congressional committees, including Alejandro Romero Gudiño and Jorge Alejandro Ortíz Ramírez of the Evaluation and Control Unit within the Vigilance Committee.

OECD is grateful to the teams from the state audit institutions of Coahuila, Puebla and Querétaro for sharing their experiences, including the auditor generals of each of these states, José Armando Plata Sandoval, David Villanueva Lomelí and Rafael Castillo Vanderpeereboom, respectively. In addition, this report benefited from the valued input of many high-level representatives of governments and Congresses at the state and municipal level in Mexico.

Table of contents

Tables

Figures

Acronyms and abbreviations

ASEC	*Auditoría Superior del Estado de Coahuila* Superior Audit of the State of Coahuila
ASEP	*Auditoría Superior del Estado de Puebla* Superior Audit of the State of Puebla
ASF	*Auditoria Superior de la Federación* Superior Audit of the Federation
ASOFIS	*Asociación Nacional de Organismos de Fiscalización Superior y Control Gubernamental* National Association of State Audit Institutions and Government Control (External)
COSO	Committee on Sponsoring Organisations of the Tredway Commission
CPCE-F	*Comisión Permanente de Contralores Estados-Federación* Permanent Commission of State Controllers-Federation
CPCP	*Comisión de Presupuesto y Cuenta Pública* Committee on Budget and Public Accounts
CVASF	*Comisión de Vigilancia de la Auditoria Superior de la Federación* Vigilance Committee of the Superior Audit of the Federation
DGFA	Director General of Forensic Audits
EFSE	*Entidades de Fiscalización Superior Estatales* State Audit Institutions
ESFEQ	*Entidad Superior de Fiscalización del Estado de Querétaro* Superior Audit of the State of Querétaro
EUROSAI	European Organisation of Supreme Audit Institutions
INTOSAI	International Organisation of Supreme Audit Institutions
ISO	International Organization for Standardization
LFRCF	*Ley de Fiscalización y Rendición de Cuentas de la Federación* Law on the Accountability and Submission of the Accounts of the Federation
OIC	*Órgano Interno de Control* Internal Control Organ
OMB	Office of Management and Budget
PAAF	*Programa Anual de Auditorías para la Fiscalización Superior de la Cuenta Pública* Annual Programme of Audits for the Public Account
SAI	Supreme Audit Institution
SFP	*Secretaria de Función Pública* Ministry of Public Administration
SNA	*Sistema Nacional Anticorrupción* National Anti-Corruption System
SNF	*Sistema Nacional de Fiscalización* National Auditing System
SNT	*Sistema Nacional de Transparencia, Acceso a la Información y Protección de Datos Personales* National Transparency System
UEC	*Unidad de Evaluación y Control* Evaluation and Control Unit

Executive summary

Moving from legislating to implementing

In May 2015, the Mexican Congress passed a series of governance reforms to enhance public sector accountability, integrity and transparency. These measures, which in some cases involved reforms to the country's Constitution, re-drew the national institutional map to advance these principles through the creation of the National Anti-Corruption System and the National Transparency System. The reforms also provide a legislative foundation for the National Auditing System (Sistema Nacional de Fiscalización, or SNF) to contribute to good governance and accountability in Mexico.

With secondary legislation passed in July 2016, the SNF now faces the challenge of implementing its mandate and demonstrating lasting impact on citizens. Mexico's supreme audit institution (SAI), the Superior Audit Office (Auditoria Superior de la Federación, or ASF), is at the forefront of these efforts as Mexico's pre-eminent external control body. The reforms expand ASF's mandate and provide it with additional tools to carry out its work, such as the ability to audit in real time, conduct investigations and report more frequently to Congress.

The effectiveness of the SNF and recent reforms also relies on other actors, including the Ministry of Public Administration, which is the federal entity responsible for internal control, as well as audit entities of states and municipalities, where legal frameworks, skills, resources, and needs are diverse. Moreover, in a system of accountability and oversight, linkages among audit institutions, the legislature, the executive branch and citizenry all influence the impact of the work of SNF members. The success of Mexico's reforms will require effective implementation and co-ordinated actions among all these actors.

Overview and proposals for action

OECD's analysis of the SNF and ASF focuses on the broader strategic considerations in a multi-system environment (Chapter 1), the national and sub-national dimensions of auditing in Mexico (Chapter 2) and the impact of ASF's work (Chapter 3). This report goes beyond an analysis of adherence to international standards, and considers the individual and co-ordinated efforts of relevant institutions for achieving governance outcomes, as illustrated by the following proposals for action:

- **The SNF could emphasise its comparative advantages for achieving policy outcomes by:**
  - further defining the SNF's short-, medium- and long-term strategic priorities and activities with a focus on its members' primary strengths in auditing, such

as providing reviews on policy coherence and the effectiveness of integrity and transparency agendas,

- dedicating an entity within the SNF, such as a new Transparency Working Group, with the primary responsibility of co-ordinating with, and defining, contributions to the National Transparency System to strengthen transparency, such as improving the effectiveness of open data initiatives.

- **ASF could refine its strategy to effectively respond to an expanded mandate and manage the risk of overextension by:**
  - communicating a clear vision, objectives and procedures with regard to its forensic audit and new investigative functions that emphasise its comparative advantage in auditing, as opposed to investigations, and help to ensure coherence with the activities of other SNF members and the Special Prosecutor for Anti-Corruption,
  - reassessing key elements of strategic and operational agility in light of new authorities, including an assessment of its strategic sensitivity, resource flexibility and leadership unity (e.g. collaboration and senior-level ownership),
  - adapting its risk-based audit programming to further prioritise how it allocates resources and reduce the volume of audits conducted.

- **The SNF could address legal, policy and implementation gaps and challenges for improved auditing and greater accountability by:**
  - strengthening the independence of sub-national audit institutions in Mexico, building on momentum of recent actions to embody the SNF in the General Law for the National Anti-corruption System,
  - advancing a coherent, government-wide approach to internal control and risk management through harmonisation of existing frameworks and improving co-ordination between external and internal audit bodies,
  - simplifying audit procedures for sub-national levels of government to minimise duplication and improve oversight of revenue-sharing transfers,
  - improving its governance structure to enhance the SNF's effectiveness, better align strategic objectives and address areas of need, particularly in municipalities,
  - increasing budgetary resources and addressing capacity gaps to help state audit institutions fulfil their mandates and mitigate the risk of disparities across regions and levels of government,
  - strengthening the professional audit service and creating sound human resource management policies in audit institutions that ensure independence and effective implementation,
  - conducting audits and evaluations that encourage ownership, accountability and skill development among public sector managers for internal control and risk management activities.

- **To ensure the relevance and impact of ASF's work, Congress could build its own technical capacity. In addition, ASF could enhance its contributions to good governance and improve uptake of its findings and recommendations by:**
  - leading government-wide studies and audits of the implementation of the National Transparency System's strategy to strengthen transparency,
  - conducting, to complement its forensic audits and investigations, evaluations of systemic deficiencies in internal control and risk management,
  - aligning its new authorities, such as the ability to start planning for audits earlier than was possible pre-reform and conducting real-time audits, with its traditional audit programming,
  - focusing its audits early in the fiscal year on high-risk programmes, as well as programme performance, in order to increase the value of reports for the budgetary decision-making process,
  - assessing its quality-control processes in order to ensure the relevance and quality of its products given new requirements to report more frequently to Congress,
  - enhancing outreach, communication strategies and training to improve relevance and impact among key stakeholders, including Congress.

Chapter 1

Designing a strategy built on the strengths of Mexico's National Auditing System (SNF)

This chapter explores strategic considerations for Mexico's National Auditing System (Sistema Nacional de Fiscalización, or SNF) and its members, to ensure effective contributions to accountability, integrity and transparency in a multi-system environment. The de jure formalisation of the SNF underscores the need for SNF members to take steps to ensure that strategic goals and objectives draw upon the strengths of individual institutions in the SNF, and clarify the system's contributions in relation to other systems based on comparative advantages. This is particularly true of Mexico's supreme audit institution, the Auditoria Superior de la Federación, which has an expanded mandate and could risk overextension in the absence of proactive efforts to balance new responsibilities and maintain its strategic agility.

Introduction

Recent constitutional reforms and accompanying secondary legislation envision three systems for advancing accountability, integrity and transparency in Mexico, including the National Anti-Corruption System (Sistema Nacional Anticorrupción, or SNA) and the National Transparency System (Sistema Nacional de Transparencia, Acceso a la Información y Protección de Datos Personales, or SNT). As part of the SNA, Mexico also formally established in law the National Auditing System (Sistema Nacional de Fiscalización, or SNF), which had existed since 2010 as a voluntary co-ordination mechanism between national and sub-national audit institutions.

The constitutional reform that led to these systems became effective in May 2015, and a key piece of legislation, the General Law for the National Anti-Corruption System, was endorsed by the Mexican government in the summer of 2016. Among other impacts, the legislation required the participation of Mexico's main control bodies in the SNF, which includes Mexico's supreme audit institution (SAI), the Superior Audit Office (Auditoria Superior de la Federación, or ASF), the Ministry of Public Administration (Secretaría de Función Pública, or SFP), which is the federal entity responsible for internal control, as well as audit entities in states and municipalities.

The *de jure* formalisation of the SNF, as well as other systems, demonstrates a significant achievement in Mexico towards greater accountability, integrity and transparency in government. The purpose of the SNF is to provide structure to the principles and activities that would support effective co-ordination among governmental audit entities of Mexico. It also aims to encourage a systematic, comprehensive approach to the auditing of public resources (ASF, 2011). The SNF fulfils this purpose based on the individual contributions, resources and commitment of its individual members. Recent reforms did not stipulate financial resources for the SNF itself as a collective body.

As Mexico shifts from legislating to implementing reforms, the SNF faces a number of strategic and operational challenges and questions. How can the SNF strategically carry out its own mandate while complementing the goals and activities of the SNA and SNT? What concrete actions can the SNF and ASF take to prepare on a strategic level for fulfilling the vision of a system-based approach to a more accountable government in Mexico? This chapter offers insights and proposals for action that help to answer these questions, drawing from international frameworks and experiences.

Table 1.1 provides a summary of the proposals for action for the SNF and ASF. The proposals are based on the idea that to ensure the effective contributions of the SNF in a multi-system environment, its members should focus on comparative advantages and clarify these relative to other systems in planning documents. This chapter provides insights and frameworks for doing this on a strategic level, and Chapter 3 further elaborates on this theme with a particular focus on ASF. The proposals for action in this chapter seek not only to aid the SNF and ASF to plan for a greater role and maximise their impact, but to help define how their roles contribute to the broader policy goals of recent reforms to strengthen accountable governance.

Table 1.1. **Proposals for action to design a strategy built on the strengths of Mexico's National Auditing System (SNF)**

Emphasising the comparative advantages of the SNF for achieving policy outcomes	The SNF could clarify its short-, medium- and long-term strategic priorities and activities based on the comparative advantage of the system and its individual actors in auditing in relation to the National Anti-Corruption System and National Transparency System, as well as policy outcomes.
	The SNF could dedicate an entity, such as a new Transparency Working Group, with the primary responsibility of co-ordinating with the National Transparency System and contributing to the effectiveness of the transparency agenda and open data initiatives.
Refining ASF's strategy to effectively respond to an expanded mandate	ASF could communicate a clear vision and objectives with regard to its forensic audit and new investigative functions that emphasise its comparative advantage in auditing and helps to ensure coherence with the activities of other SNF members and the Special Prosecutor for Anti-Corruption.
	ASF could ensure its ability to effectively balance and respond to new responsibilities by conducting an in-depth review of key elements of its strategic and operational agility, including an assessment of its strategic sensitivity, resource flexibility and leadership unity.
	ASF could adapt its risk-based audit programming to further prioritise how it allocates resources and reduce the volume of audits conducted.

Emphasising the comparative advantages of the National Auditing System for achieving policy outcomes

The SNF could further define its short-, medium- and long-term strategic priorities and activities with a focus on its members' primary strengths in auditing.

The SNF has existed as a voluntary co-ordination mechanism between internal and external audit institutions across levels of government since 2010. The purpose of the SNF was and continues to be to provide structure to the principles and activities that would support effective co-ordination among Mexico's governmental audit entities. It also aims to foster a systematic, comprehensive approach to the auditing of public resources (ASF, 2011). Table 1.2 summarises the roles of key actors in the SNF.

Table 1.2. **The role of key actors in Mexico's National Auditing System (SNF)**

SNF members	Description
Supreme Audit Institution (Auditoria Superior de la Federación, or ASF)	ASF is "organically dependent" on the Chamber of Deputies of Mexico, which is the lower house of the bicameral legislature of Mexico (Article 79 of the Constitution [Government of Mexico, 1917). The Constitution grants ASF technical, managerial and functional autonomy, even though it belongs to the Chamber of Deputies, which is formally vested with the country's auditing function. As a consequence, ASF is neither a constitutional power nor an independent constitutional organ, but rather a "constitutionally-relevant organ" (UNAM, 2007; Ackerman, 2006). ASF has numerous responsibilities to provide external oversight for public accounts, management and safekeeping of resources, devising recommendations based on audits to improve government functions and reporting to Congress on findings, among other duties.
Ministry of Public Administration (Secretaría de Función Pública, or SFP)	The SFP is a federal executive entity in charge of organising and co-ordinating the governmental control and evaluation system through the internal control bodies established within each line ministry. For instance, the SFP defines the norms for the federal public administration's control procedures, and establishes the basis for audits in all the agencies and entities of the federal administration. It also monitors federal public servants to ensure they adhere to the law when exercising their functions, and penalises those who fail to do so. The SFP has other responsibilities, such as promoting compliance with control processes and determining procurement policy.
State Audit Institutions (Entidades Fiscalizadoras Superiores Locales, or EFSL)	Mexico is a federal system composed of 31 states and an autonomous entity (Mexico City), which are all granted constitutional recognition. The federal government exercises supreme power throughout Mexico, but states and Mexico City have their own independent governments, budgets and auditing systems managed by the 32 EFSL. The 32 EFSL, together with ASF, form the National Association of State Audit Institutions and Government Control (Asociación Nacional de Organismos de Fiscalización Superior y Control Gubernamental, or ASOFIS) for external audit entities.
State ministries responsible for internal controls and audit	Internal control agencies (*contralorias*) in each state government are responsible for internal control and audit, with duties similar to SFP at the federal level. The co-ordination mechanism for these institutions is the National Permanent Commission of State Controllers (Comisión Permanente de Contralores Estados-Federación, or CPCE-F), chaired by SFP.
Municipal controllers and internal control units of constitutionally independent entities	The internal control and audit offices of public sector organisations recognised in the Constitution, yet are outside of the federal government administration.

Note: Other audit entities exist in Mexico, such as controllers in the judicial and legislative branches. Membership to SNF is open to all internal and external audit bodies in the executive, legislative or judicial branches, as well as all levels of government (federal, state and municipal).

Source: Government of Mexico (2015), "Ley General de Transparencia y Acceso a la Información Pública" [General Law on Transparency and Access to Public Information], *Diario Oficial de la Federación*, 4 May 2015, www.dof.gob.mx/nota_detalle.php?codigo=5391143 &fecha=04/05/2015; Government of Mexico (2016a), "Ley General de Responsabilidades Administrativas" [General Law of Administrative Responsibilities], *Diario Oficial de la Federación*, 18 July, www.dof.gob.mx/nota_detalle.php?codigo=5391143&fecha=04/05/2015.

In October 2012, SNF members approved a strategic plan that spans from 2013 to 2017. The strategy consists of five high-level principles: co-ordination of effective work, strengthening institutions, avoiding duplication and gaps, increased coverage of control for public resources at federal and local levels, and issuing of relevant reports that are simple and accessible. In addition, the plan communicates the following goals, each of which has its own set of specific objectives and actions:

- common professional standards nationwide
- capacity building
- exchange information and joint work
- improve the legal and operational framework related to auditing
- increased impact of the work of auditing institutions in the fight against corruption
- strengthen the role of auditing within the "system of promotion, determination and establishment of responsibilities" for public officials (ASF, 2011).

To further align its activities following recent reforms and the establishment of the National Anti-Corruption System (Sistema Nacional Anticorrupción, or SNA) and the National Transparency System (Sistema Nacional de Transparencia, Acceso a la Información y Protección de Datos Personales, or SNT), SNF could update its strategic plan to clarify its comparative advantages in relation to these systems. Refining the strategy and identifying advantages at the system level can aid individual SNF members to make necessary strategic changes at the institutional level, thereby promoting coherence. Doing so will be critical for actors to maximise their contributions and avoid overextension. This is particularly true of ASF, which will feature prominently in all three systems to strengthen accountability, integrity and transparency (see Table 1.3).

Table 1.3. **The National Anti-Corruption System and the National Transparency System**

National Anti-Corruption System (Sistema Nacional Anticorrupción, or SNA)	**Overview**: SNA is a co-ordinating body for all the authorities of any governmental order dealing with corruption and notably, "with the auditing and the control of public resources" (Article 113 of the Mexican Constitution). The system will have a co-ordinating committee (see below for stakeholders), which will be responsible for steering the design and implementation of anti-corruption policies and mechanisms. States will need to establish anti-corruption systems to co-ordinate with local authorities on matters related to corruption.
	Stakeholders: SNA consists of the new Administrative Justice Tribunal (Tribunal Federal de Justicia Administrativa), the new Anti-Corruption Prosecutor (Fiscalía Anti-corrupción), the Ministry of Public Administration (Secretaria de la Función Pública, or SFP), the Federal Judicial Council (Consejo de la Judicatura Federal) and a representative from the Citizen Participation Committee.
	ASF's role: ASF is expected to contribute significantly to the SNA Co-ordination Committee (Comité Coordinador del Sistema Nacional Anticorrupción) and, in particular, to conduct its audit-related tasks assigned to in the Constitution, including: 1) the design and promotion of comprehensive policies on auditing and control of public resources, 2) the establishment of a common basis and principles for the effective co-ordination of the authorities of any level in relation to auditing and control of public resources; and 3) the elaboration of non-binding recommendations to improve performance and internal control based on the yearly report, which will be drafted by the Committee (Article 113, 2015).
National Transparency System (Sistema Nacional de Transparencia, Acceso a la Información y Protección de Datos Personales, or SNT)	**Overview**: The General Law on Transparency creates the SNT, and sets out 50 obligations for proactive transparency of certain information for states, and gives Mexico's National Institute for Transparency and Access to Information to Public Information, and Data Protection (El Instituto Nacional de Transparencia, Acceso a la Información y Protección de Datos Personales, or INAI) and other relevant entities sanction powers for noncompliance. Among other things, the law also creates a National Transparency Platform (Platforma Nacional de Transparencia) that will allow users to request information. Some of the core functions of the SNT include promoting policies, research, and analysis on matters of transparency, access to information, protection of personal data and open government. The SNT is also meant to promote citizen participation and digitisation of information.
	Stakeholders: The SNT is comprised of INAI, ASF, the General National Archive (El Archivo General de la Nación), and the National Institute of Statistics and Geography (El Instituto Nacional de Estadística y Geografía).
	ASF's role: The role of ASF in the SNT has been defined in internal regulations.* In particular, ASF has been called to lead the SNT's Auditing Commission, which is given specific co-ordination and analytical tasks, including to establish coherence with the work of the SNF. The reforms envision that the auditing results and reports will be published for any government entities that are subject to auditing by law. However, it also provides for the possibility to classify as "confidential" information that may "obstruct the verification, inspection and auditing activities related to implementation of laws, or affect the collection of taxes" (Article 113, 2015).

Note: *These regulations (ASF, 2013) include the Regulation of the National Council of the National Transparency System (Reglamento del Consejo Nacional del Sistema Nacional de Transparencia, Acceso a la Información Pública y Protección de Datos Personales), the Access to Public Information and Protection of Personal Data (Acceso a la Información Pública y Protección de Datos Personales); Guidelines for the organisation, co-ordination and operation of the bodies of the members of the National Transparency System (Lineamientos para la organización, coordinación y funcionamiento de las instancias de los integrantes del Sistema Nacional de Transparencia, Acceso a la Información Pública y Protección de Datos Personales), and the Work Programme of the Commission for Accountability (Programa de Trabajo de la Comisión de Rendición de Cuentas).

Source: Government of Mexico (2015), "Ley General de Transparencia y Acceso a la Información Pública" [General Law on Transparency and Access to Public Information], *Diario Oficial de la Federación*, 4 May 2015, www.dof.gob.mx/nota_detalle.php?codigo=5391143&fecha=04/05/2015; Government of Mexico (2016a), "Ley General de Responsabilidades Administrativas" [General Law of Administrative Responsibilities], *Diario Oficial de la Federación*, 18 July, www.dof.gob.mx/nota_detalle.php?codigo=5391143&fecha=04/05/2015.

SNF's strategy documents provide a foundation for its stakeholders, but can be updated to align better with recent reforms. The documents articulate broad objectives, define certain roles for individual stakeholders or working groups and promote co-ordination across systems. For example, SNF's Basis for Operations (Bases Operativas para el Funcionamiento del SNF), assigns the SNF's Governing Committee (Comité Rector) with the task of co-ordinating with the SNA, and it assigns the SNF's Legal Working Group the goal of elaborating and adopting common measures with respect to the SNA (ASF, 2015a).[1] However, given the time period it covers (2013-17), the SNF's strategic plan does not address its role within the SNA. In addition, neither SNF's strategy nor its Basis for Operations addresses the role of the SNF and its stakeholders relative to co-ordination and interactions with the SNT. As Box 1.1 illustrates, recognising the linkages between actors and codependencies between systems, including the SNF and SNT, is critical for achieving policy outcomes.

Box 1.1. **Linking systems of accountability and transparency: "Subsidios al Campo" in Mexico**

In 2008, a coalition between civil society organisations and interest groups launched an online platform called "Subsidios al Campo en México," or Farm Subsidies in Mexico (Subsidios, www.subsidiosalcampo.org.mx). The coalition launched the website as an online tool to strengthen transparency by disclosing information and data on federal farm subsidies. The website also includes aggregate data on subsidies by state, municipality and region, as well as across years and types of programmes. The information is presented dynamically on the website, using graphics, figures and maps to aid comprehension and comparative analysis. According to the website, the initiative aimed to systematise information from different sources (state secretariats, decentralised agencies, research centres and media) with the goal of:

- ensuring transparency of rural budgets by identifying beneficiaries, amounts and location of subsidies
- promoting the right of access to public information by the Federal Law of Transparency and Access to Public Government Information
- promoting accountability by the agencies, decision makers and public servants responsible for federal agricultural policy
- facilitating dialogue on public policies and rural development.

Since 2008, the website has become a valuable source of information for analysis and news reports, attracting over 20 million searches according to the website counter. By various measures, Subsidios has been a successful initiative to strengthen transparency; however, challenges existed stemming from underlying assumptions about the linkages and inter-reliance between transparency and accountability mechanisms and actors. The assumptions included:

- Public and accessible information would be used by civil society organisations and the citizenry to demand government action.
- Key accountability actors involved in agricultural policy, including the supreme audit institution (Auditoría Superior de la Federación, ASF, the Ministry of Public Administration and Congress) would be responsive to the demands of citizenry, and use the information to improve oversight functions.
- The Executive Branch, including the Ministry of Agriculture, would be equally responsive to the findings and recommendations of accountability actors, leading to the adoption of policy changes.

Box 1.1. **Linking systems of accountability and transparency: "Subsidios al Campo" in Mexico** *(continued)*

In the years leading up to the Subsidios initiative, Mexico had undergone significant political and institutional change to strengthen accountability. This included the creation of ASF in 2000, as well as passage of federal legislation establishing freedom of information in 2002 and the inclusion of access to government information rights in the Mexican Constitution in 2007 (Cejudo, 2012). Nonetheless, a study of Subsidios noted that the accountability institutions did not always carry out their duties when Subsidios alerted them to problems because of disjointed accountability mechanisms, lack of incentives and limited institutional capacity (Cejudo, 2012).

Transparency without accountability can come in various forms. In the case of Subsidios, the innovative transparency initiative of an online portal was generally a success, but key users of the information (i.e. accountability actors) did not have the incentives or capacity to use the information. Traditional pitfalls of online transparency policies also include barriers to information access and the resistance of government entities to exposure from public disclosure (Shkabatur, 2012). Barriers to information access involve not only public disclosure of information (quantity), but also the manner in which it is disclosed (quality) and whether the public or accountability actors can analyse and understand the information.

The assumptions in the case of Subsidios illustrate the important linkages between transparency initiatives and accountability mechanisms. Systems of transparency rely on systems of accountability to achieve certain outcomes, and vice versa. As illustrated by the assumptions in the case of Subsidios, actors within a system of accountability have responsibilities to respond to transparency initiatives in order to affect policy change. When refining its strategy relative to the other systems, SNF can consider this linkage and its own role and engagement with the National Transparency System. In addition, as discussed in the next section, SNF members can consider their contributions to the transparency agenda. This can include reviews of the architecture of transparency policies, and whether they are designed and implemented to avoid traditional pitfalls of transparency policies.

Source: Cejudo, G. M. (2012), "Evidence for change: The case of Subsidios al Campo in Mexico", *Study No. 6*, International Budget Partnership, www.internationalbudget.org/wp-content/uploads/LP-case-study-Fundar.pdf; Shkabatur, J. (2012), "Transparency with(out) accountability: Open government in the United States", *Yale Law & Policy Review*, 31(1), 79-140, www.jstor.org/stable/23735771; Subsidios al Campo (n.d.), "About this project", webpage, http://subsidiosalcampo.org.mx/acerca-de/sobre-este-proyecto/ (accessed 31 May 2016).

SNF and its members could take additional steps towards refining and implementing a strategy beyond 2017, including designing an action plan with clearly defined objectives, outputs and outcomes for the short-, medium- and long-term. The current strategy and Basis for Operations focuses primarily on activities that reflect outputs (e.g. common professional standards nationwide) and the activities that serve those outputs (e.g. adoption of manuals, guidelines and common supervisory work of SNF members). Strategic documents could better reflect SNF's collective strengths as a system of accountability actors, considering the goals, potential co-ordination and duplication with other systems (i.e. SNA and SNT), as well as policy outcomes. Strategic and outcome-oriented considerations for the SNF include the following:

- **Provide an overarching perspective on the policy coherence and co-ordination of integrity and transparency agendas across government, as well as institutional arrangements, to ensure outcomes**. Policy coherence is not only a function of co-ordination, effectiveness or value for money, it is about integrated policy design and implementation towards the achievement of outcomes. The SNF can contribute to greater policy coherence through reviews, audits, and strategic co-ordination with other systems, as discussed in Chapter 3. Moreover, the SNF and its members themselves are instruments of policy coherence.

- **Ensure effective design and implementation of integrity and transparency policies through audits and related advisory work at multiple levels of government**. Unlike the previous bullet, this activity focuses more on performance of individual institutions to implement a particular policy or programme, as opposed to the coherence of policies. Addressing these particular areas from a strategic perspective can provide a foundation for individual SNF members to define and align their audit programming with broader strategic priorities of the system. As discussed further in Chapter 3, ASF in particular has a comparative advantage in reviewing the design and implementation of transparency policies.
- **Enhance integrity through reviews of systemic internal control deficiencies and support of investigations of fraud and corruption, emphasising prevention over detection**. The comparative advantage of audit institutions in strengthening integrity is to review and evaluate the root of problems that can have ramifications for policy design and implementation across a ministry or government as a whole. In this respect, they have the mandate, skills and knowledge to go beyond investigation of individual cases, as a complement to law enforcement and other investigatory bodies (see Chapter 3 for additional analysis).
- **Model principles of accountability, integrity and transparency in the strategies and operations of SNF as a whole, as well as individual SNF members**. Existing SNF publications recognise the value of modelling these principles. For instance, the "General Information of the SNF" publication notes that transparency is one of the most important aspects for exercising oversight, and that SNF members should take steps to promote transparency, such as publicly disclosing audit information and expeditiously exchanging information to facilitate audits (SNF, 2015). Recognition of their own role for achieving broader goals of accountability, integrity and transparency is critical for the SNF to continue to reflect in future strategy documents.

The secondary legislation will help SNF members to refine their roles and strategies; however, the legal mandate alone may not fully define comparative advantages, since advantage can also be a function of capacity or position to act relative to other actors (UNDG, 2009). For example, as noted above, ASF is well-positioned to improve the prevention of fraud and corruption by providing analyses and recommendations to address internal control deficiencies related to its investigations of corruption or wrongdoing. Such considerations reflect strategic choices and how an entity decides to use its new authority in practice.

Finally, in order for the SNF's strategic plan to be effective, better alignment between the strategic goals and objectives of individual SNF members, including the CPCE-F and ASOFIS, and the SNF itself, is needed. SNF leadership could ensure that each organisation's respective strategic plans are aligned with the broader SNF strategic plan. Consideration could be given to the specific issues that each body is set to address or examine, bearing in mind that in unique circumstances some overlap and duplication may be reasonable for achieving overall strategic goals and outcomes.

The SNF could dedicate an entity, such as a new Transparency Working Group, with the primary responsibility of co-ordinating with the National Transparency System and contributing to the effectiveness of the transparency agenda and open data initiatives.

As audit institutions, SNF members are responsible for promoting transparency in their external interactions and internal operations. Their responsibilities are reflected in the International Organisation of Supreme Audit Institutions' (INTOSAI's) international principles for transparency. Specifically, audit institutions are obliged to publicise audit findings and conclusions, as well as grant public access to information. They should also act as models for transparency with regard to publicly reporting on their inner workings (e.g. strategy, operations and performance) in a timely, reliable, clear manner (INTOSAI 2010). As noted above, SNF's own guidelines call for its members to be models for transparency.

Adhering to the principles of transparency in practice can take many forms for the SNF and its stakeholders. One common way for all SNF members is to consider the substance and quality of interactions with key stakeholders, including the citizenry. This notion is reflected in various external and internal control standards, largely with respect to standards for ensuring the timelines, quality, and readability of audit reports. Additional considerations include transparency and communication related to the audit institutions mission, strategy and activities in order to improve understanding within government and the community at large about SAIs' activities (see Annex 1.A1 for an example from the State of Puebla).

Such actions in the spirit of transparency are critical and constitute some of the fundamental ways audit institutions can contribute to transparency. These efforts go hand-in-hand with other common ways for organisations, including audit institutions, to promote transparency, such as creating online portals to report on results and support open data. For instance, Chile's Office of the Comptroller General of the Republic of Chile (CGR), introduced an online portal in 2014, which provides a forum for the articulation, storage, consultation and publication of the information on the investment of resource in public works. Its ultimate aim is to promote social control and citizen-driven accountability by providing reliable and timely information that is useful for analysing and monitoring resources invested in public works. In addition, ASF has its own online portal (Public System of Consultation of Audits, or Sistema Público de Consultas de Auditorías), which allows citizens to access historical information from audits of public accounts since 2000 based on various criterion, such as the fiscal year, audited entity, themes and observations. The portal consolidates ASF's databases, and supports the user experience with tables, graphics, exportable Excel files, an operational guide and tutorials.[2]

SNF and its individual members have taken steps to strengthen transparency and engagement with citizenry, but opportunities remain to improve its strategic approach in light of the National Transparency System (Sistema Nacional de Transparencia, Acceso a la Información y Protección de Datos Personales, or SNT). Moreover, ASF will play a key role in both the SNF and SNT, underscoring the important linkages between the principles of accountability and transparency the two systems represent. To consolidate internal efforts and ensure a strategic, co-ordinated approach to transparency issues, SNF could dedicate an entity with these responsibilities, or establish a Transparency Working Group. If the latter, this group would complement existing working groups for professional auditing standards, legal and consulting issues, internal controls, accounting and social participation (see Chapter 2 for additional details on the working groups). The working group could also help SNF to refine its broader short-, medium- and long-term strategy for co-ordinating with the SNT and contributing to policy outcomes for greater transparency in Mexico. In addition, the working group would allow for a targeted approach for SNF members to overcome challenges in an ever-changing environment to uphold the principles of transparency.

One challenging area that deserves strategic attention is the increasingly data-driven environment in which the government operates. Innovations in both the private and public sectors to digitise information places pressure on audit institutions to maintain capacity, expertise, and infrastructure to effectively use and disseminate data. To evolve with this environment, and effectively contribute to transparency, SNF members can explore opportunities to be more effective consumers and producers (i.e. prosumers) of open data. Open data initiatives can build on other approaches to improved transparency, like clear and timely reporting on audit results and maintaining an effective online presence.

OECD's work on open data, as discussed in Box 1.2, provides some context to inform the strategic thinking of the Transparency Working Group, on its potential role, and activities in this area. Key strategic questions for the group, particularly ASF given its broad mandate and role in external auditing, include the following:

- What are the opportunities, challenges and solutions for audit institutions to be consumers of open data, incorporating them as inputs into audit processes?
- What are the opportunities, challenges and solutions for audit institutions to be contributors to the open data ecosystem?
- How might the current legal framework create limitations on audit institutions as contributors to open data initiatives, since they may not "own" the data they use? Are there ways to overcome these limitations?
- What policies and processes, as well as skills and structures, do audit entities need to adopt in order to become better prosumers of open data and effectively contribute to Mexico's transparency agenda?
- How can audit institutions contribute to improving the design and implementation of open data policies through their traditional audit programming? (See next section for further discussion.)

Box 1.2. Improving transparency through open data initiatives and auditing

Open government data (OGD), as a component of open data, is a philosophy - and increasingly a set of policies - that promotes transparency, accountability and value creation by making government data available to all. Public bodies produce and commission large quantities of data and information. By making their datasets available, public institutions become more transparent and accountable to citizens. By encouraging the use, reuse and free distribution of datasets, governments promote business creation and innovative, citizen-centric services. OGD has the potential to increase government efficiency, effectiveness and innovation in service delivery and internal public sector operations. The following are key definitions related to OGD, which is an input for open data.

- **Open data**: Data that can be freely used, re-used and distributed by anyone, only subject to (at the most) the requirement that users attribute the data and that they make their work available to be shared as well. Open data is not OGD, as the latter is government data that is made public in open formats.

Box 1.2. Improving transparency through open data initiatives and auditing *(continued)*

- **Public sector information**: Information, including information products and services, generated, created, collected, processed, preserved, maintained, disseminated, or funded by, or for, a government or public institution.
- **Big data**: A data-driven socio-economic model; as a phenomenon emerged as available datasets produced by various sources have grown larger and data users more aware of the value obtainable through linked and combined datasets produced by different actors, both private and public.

By making their data available, easily accessible and reusable by citizens and businesses, governments can improve accountability and transparency, create new business opportunities and better inform both citizen engagement and their own decision making. For instance, data should be available where they are needed, in the format they are needed. Data need to be secure, and confidentiality and privacy of those providing the data protected, especially where there is information about individuals. Moreover, externally, the organisation should be perceived as treating data responsibly.

For ASF, as compared to other SNF members, how it might contribute to transparency through its external audit function is an important strategic consideration. The promotion of accountability through oversight remains a core activity of supreme audit institutions' (SAIs') work. However, as an unpublished OECD survey of ten SAIs showed, they are increasingly using their expertise to provide insight and foresight to drive improvements across government related to open government data. For instance, SAIs are conducting audits and evaluations in a range of areas that focus on the effective use of data in government, such as those that focus on accessibility and reliability of data systems for collecting, storing and using performance information.

In addition, internal control bodies like SFP also conduct work in similar areas that advance OGD principles. For example, internal control standards incorporate a number of open data principles into their audits that are meant to ensure the quality of information. In line with international standards, internal control bodies review the infrastructure for processing data, assess the reliability of data sources, and determine whether processes for converting data into quality information are effective, among other things.

Source: Ubaldi, B. (2013), "Open government data: Towards empirical analysis of open government data initiatives", *OECD Working Papers on Public Governance*, No. 22, OECD Publishing, Paris, http://dx.doi.org/10.1787/5k46bj4f03s7-en; OECD (2014a), "Rebooting public service delivery – How can open government data help to drive innovation?", www.oecd.org/gov/digital-government/rebooting-public-service-delivery.htm; OECD (2016), *Supreme Audit Institutions and Good Governance: Oversight, Insight and Foresight*, OECD Publishing, Paris, http://dx.doi.org/10.1787/9789264263871-en.

The answers to the strategic questions above will vary by SNF member, since differences in mandates, mission and expertise influence how the strategy will translate into an action plan. For instance, ASF is in the best position to conduct government-wide reviews of the transparency agenda, including any open data initiatives, given its role and powers as Mexico's SAI (see Chapter 3). Moreover, the legal framework creates certain parameters for audit institutions to take specific actions to strengthen transparency. As one example, the General Law on Transparency and Access to Information (Ley Federal de Transparencia y Acceso a la Información Pública Gubernamental) requires ASF, and other institutions, to comply with transparency and access to information obligations contained in its articles, including generating, documenting and publishing information in an accessible and open format. In addition, audit institutions can have legal and operational limitations for how they access and use data from other entities, as discussed above. This can limit their contributions to an open data ecosystem, as they may not be the "owners" of the data they use, and therefore much of the financial and nonfinancial information they might contribute to an ecosystem are derivative of original sources.

The entity responsible for coherence and co-ordination with the National Transparency System can assist the SNF in addressing such limitations in a strategic, consistent way. Moreover, it could provide a platform for audit institutions, and ASF in particular, to contribute to transparency without overextending itself by taking on a major leadership role in the SNT itself. Within audit institutions, there is more to transparency than providing access to information, making it searchable or presenting it attractively, such as using plain language or creating simple web interfaces (OECD, 2014a). Specifically, transparency initiatives of audit institutions could consider a strategy that not only defines the what (right data), when (right time) and how (design) of the data, but also the monitoring of, and improvements to, its actual use. A dedicated entity, or a Transparency Working Group, would help SNF members to be better models for transparency through a co-ordinated approach. In addition, the entity could be a forum for SNF members to identify and share their experiences with regard to auditing transparency policies across government, as explored in Chapter 3.

Refining ASF's strategy to effectively respond to an expanded mandate

ASF could communicate a clear vision, objectives and procedures with regard to its forensic audit and new investigative functions that emphasise its comparative advantage in auditing and help to ensure coherence with the activities of other SNF members and the Special Prosecutor for Anti-Corruption.

Since 2009, ASF has conducted forensic audits to combat fraud and corruption identified during audits of the year-end account (see Chapter 3 for a detailed discussion of this capacity). As a separate function, the General Law of Administrative Responsibilities, amended and endorsed in July 2016 (entering into force in 2017), grants ASF the authority to conduct investigations and substantiate "grave" administrative irregularities, or "faltas administrativas graves" (Government of Mexico, 2016b). The Law on the Accountability and Submission of the Accounts of the Federation (Ley de Fiscalización y Rendición de Cuentas de la Federación, or LRCF), also approved in July 2016, requires ASF to establish two separate departments for carrying these duties, including one for conducting investigations and one for substantiation of cases (Government of Mexico, 2016b). The Federal Tribunal of Administrative Justice (Tribunal Federal de Justicia Administrativa), based on the evidence submitted by ASF, is responsible for adjudicating the cases and making decisions as to whether they warrant administrative sanctions. The Special Prosecutor for Anti-Corruption, created as part of recent reforms, will investigate and adjudicate cases of potential criminal offences (Government of Mexico, 2016a). Moreover, the ministries and the Organs of Internal Control, as well as their counterparts in the states, will investigate and substantiate administrative offenses that are "not grave," i.e. "faltas administrativas no graves" (Government of Mexico, 2016a).

Notwithstanding its new authorities for investigation and substantiation, ASF's comparative advantage lies first and foremost in its audit function. ASF's auditors have familiarity with public accounts that no other governmental actor has. If ASF is to take on additional responsibilities for investigating cases, even if they are geared towards administrative cases, it is critical for the strategic plan for 2018 and beyond to communicate this advantage and demonstrate clear goals and direction. ASF's current strategic plan for 2011 to 2017 states generally that forensic auditing is an area it intends to strengthen, but the vision and objectives behind this role, including its connection to ASF's broader strategic objectives, is undeveloped. Moreover, since reforms only recently expanded ASF's authority to conduct investigations related to potential administrative wrongdoing, as well as substantiation, the strategic plan does not directly address this new role. An updated plan would help ASF make decisions about resource allocation and capacity development, as well as reduce strategic, operational and reputational risks:

- **Resource allocation**: ASF's investigative and substantiation caseload will grow not only because of its expanded mandate, but also as a result of greater publicity in this area, which can lead to increased volume of complaints and allegations. Investigations can be resource-intensive to implement. A strategy that explicitly acknowledges investigative goals and objectives is the first step to effective prioritisation of work and efficient resource allocation. Indeed, without an increase in budgetary resources, trade-offs to fulfil any investigative role are likely. In contemplating the trade-offs, a strategic approach that emphasises ASF's core strengths and does not compromise its traditional auditing role will be critical for effective implementation of new authorities.
- **Knowledge, expertise, and infrastructure**: Investigations require specialised knowledge, skills, and technical capacity (e.g. case management databases) that ASF would need to develop for it to be effective. Moreover, a broader investigative role, even for administrative wrongdoing, could unexpectedly lead to the discovery of criminal behaviour. The substantiation of administrative cases follows different standards than audits. Moreover, they require expertise in investigative processes to ensure high evidentiary quality to decide on potential sanctions. ASF officials highlighted the need for qualified staff in this area.
- **Strategic and operational risk**:[3] ASF's comparative advantage, relative to other audit institutions and anti-corruption entities, is its external control function and expertise in auditing. How its expanded investigative power is aligned and balanced with this traditional audit role remains to be seen, both from a strategic and operational perspective. The strategic plan should help ASF to set objectives for its investigations and meet external demands without compromising its primary role as an independent external control body, thereby reducing strategic risk (see next section for further discussion). Operational risk can include the uncertainty resulting from ineffective relationships or co-ordination between ASF teams (e.g. investigative and audit teams), as well as ASF and other SNF members responsible for auditing the effectiveness of internal control systems, such as the SFP.
- **Reputational risk**: This refers to the potential for ASF's actions to lead to a negative perception about its capability or credibility. Investigations of potential wrongdoing carry reputational risks, both internally and externally, given the publicity and political sensitivities that can surround them. Moreover, investigations can have internal spill over effects that may be positive and negative on the public perception of ASF's traditional audit work. As such, the perceived legitimacy and credibility of ASF's core activities are positively correlated with perception of how effectively it uses and implements its new investigative authority.

ASF's approach to both its forensic audits, as well as its new roles to conduct investigations and substantiation, has implications for other institutions that are responsible for the investigation and adjudication of fraud and corruption cases. In addition to a clear vision and objectives related to its forensic audit and investigative functions, ASF, and others, could develop procedures to ensure effective coherence and co-ordination with other institutions with investigative roles. This includes the Federal Tribunal of Administrative Justice and the Special Prosecutor for Anti-Corruption, as discussed.

Such procedures are especially beneficial for cases that are ambiguous in terms of whether they are "grave," recognising also that investigations can involve elements of both administrative and criminal wrongdoing. In some circumstances, a joint investigation, or mechanisms for ongoing consultations throughout an investigation, could be appropriate. Procedures that further define and streamline these processes will help to ensure coherence of the individual efforts of multiple institutions with common purposes.

ASF could ensure its ability to effectively balance and respond to new responsibilities by conducting an in-depth review of key elements of its strategic and operational agility, including an assessment of its strategic sensitivity, resource flexibility and leadership unity.

The success of ASF's strategic planning in the coming years is dependent on its ability to leverage its comparative advantage in the National Auditing System (Sistema Nacional de Fiscalización, or SNF), while balancing competing priorities of the three systems and avoiding overextension. In the wake of recent reforms, ASF's mandate is set to expand significantly. Without a budget increase or identification of efficiencies, taking on additional responsibilities may be unsustainable. The risk of overextension stems from the following reforms, in particular:

- ASF will play a leading role in three systems, which will include responsibilities on the co-ordination committees of the SNF, the SNA and the SNT.
- The possibility for ASF to audit entities in relation to the ongoing fiscal year (so-called "real-time" audits), and substantially, to audit revenue sharing (i.e. *participaciones*) given to states as well as the revenues made by sub-national entities through loans guaranteed by the central government (see Chapter 2 for more details).
- The obligation to report its activity to Congress three times a year (June, October, and February), including the General Executive Report to be submitted for consideration to the plenary of Congress. In addition, twice a year (the first of May and November), ASF will also report to Congress about its follow-up activities, such as the amount of compensations paid by audited entities as a consequence of ASF's recommendations (see Chapter 3 for more details).
- The mandate to investigate and substantiate, together with the internal control entities, the serious administrative offences cases, which are then adjudicated by the new Federal Tribunal of Administrative Justice (Tribunal Federal de Justicia Administrativa) responsible for imposing sanctions.

To meet the new demands related to ASF's audit work, ASF could consider its strategic and operational agility, as well as its strengths and weaknesses in relation to other actors responsible for the anti-corruption, accountability and transparency agendas. The concept of strategic agility derives from the private sector, which has similarly faced challenges related to rapid change, convergence of activities across areas and the rise of networks. Research on success factors identified three elements that, taken together, allow an organisation to be strategically agile, as shown in Figure 1.1. Operational agility refers to the ability of ASF to align resources to changing priorities and to promote innovative ways to maximise performance (OECD, 2014b).

Maintaining the strategic and operational agility of ASF in an evolving environment means adapting resources to fulfil its new mandate and taking innovative approaches in light of constraints. It also highlights the need for ASF to strategically consider opportunities to build its internal capacity in preparation for effectively responding to its new mandate. This report provides proposals for action for ASF (and SNF) to enhance strategic and operational agility within a confined scope, but additional actions can be taken on their own in light of an evolving policy environment. Figure 1.1 provides a framework for assessing strategic agility.

Figure 1.1. **Key elements and drivers for assessing strategy agility**

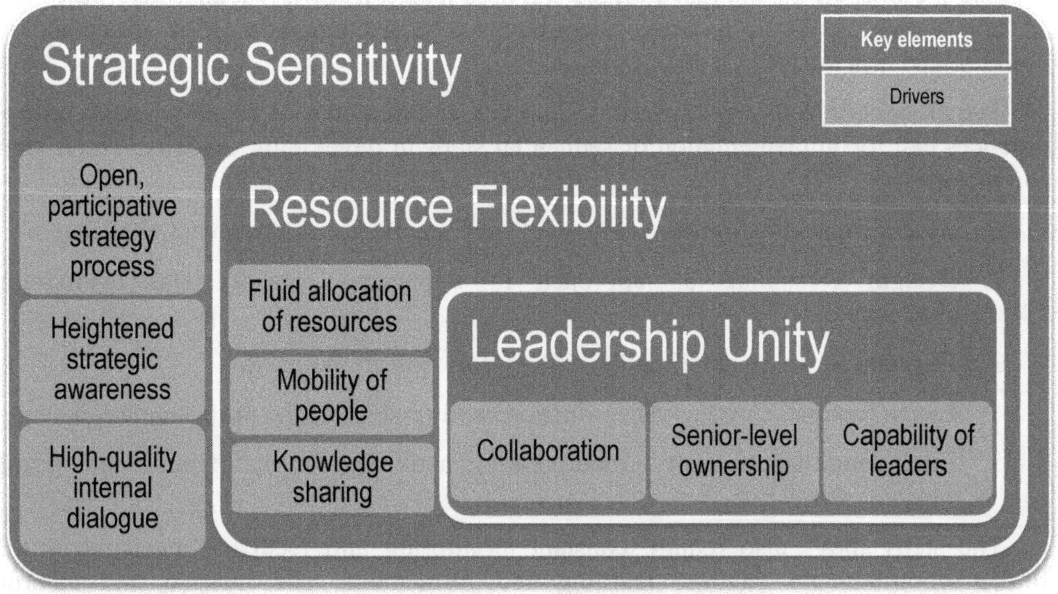

Source: Adapted from OECD (2011), "International Workshop 'Strategic Agility for Strong Societies and Economies': Summary and issues for further debate'', unclassified document, OECD Public Governance Committee, www.oecd.org/officialdocuments/publicdisplaydocumentpdf/?cote=GOV/PGC/PGR(2012)1&docLanguage=En.

ASF's current strategic plan spans from 2011 to 2017 and will soon need updating. This provides an opportunity for ASF to set new priorities for its activities in light of recent reforms that focus not just on its role in the SNF, but across all three systems. In addition, these priorities will need balancing against ASF's expanded mandate for its own work. Of paramount concern is ASF's ability to maintain its operational agility and identify its comparative advantages and priorities at a strategic level, taking into account its auditing, organisational, and external relations capacities.

Strengths to consider could include ASF's independence, its reputation for being trustworthy, and its unique overarching view of the public sector and governance issues. Potential weaknesses could include limitations with regard to the type of audits conducted (e.g. emphasis on financial and compliance audits over performance audits), as well as limited capacity and experience for conducting investigations. Subsequent chapters will further explore these strategic considerations in greater detail with regard to specific goals and authorities of the SNF and ASF outlined in recent reforms.

In thinking about its operational agility, in particular, examination of the internal capacity and structural aspects of ASF would be critical and timely. Such an examination can include a review of ASF's audit capacity, organisational capacity and its ability to manage the external environment. Other relevant areas for review are operating structures, internal control schemes, procedures of redistributing human and technical resources, and development of management tools. In addition, ASF could consider the strengths and weaknesses of other audit institutions, such as SFP, since external control often relies on, or is directly influenced by, the quality of internal control and internal audit functions. For instance, in the Netherlands it is the responsibility of the internal audit department to audit financial statements, as well as financial and operational management systems. The Netherlands Court of Audits (NCA) has a system whereby it reviews the work of the internal auditors and uses that in its own risk analysis. If the work of the internal auditors is done according to NCA standards, it is accepted and incorporated into the NCA's audit opinion.

The process of assessing capacity should not be completed on an ad hoc basis, as best practices call for implementation of sequential steps in developing capacity. Those steps can include:

1. **Assess**: Assessing the current state of ASF's capacity, and relevant challenges.
2. **Design**: Designing an approach to improving capacity and overcoming challenges.
3. **Implement**: Implementing the strategy for capacity building.
4. **Learn lessons**: Conducting evaluations and reviews of the implementation.
5. **Institutionalise capacity**: Incorporating activities for maintaining the desired capacity level.

The steps above also require constant monitoring and feedback mechanisms that further contribute to ongoing learning and refinement. The internal and external environment is fluid and subject to ongoing changes, and therefore the capacity-building efforts must be systematically undertaken and flexible to effectively respond to changes. Key aspects of capacity building, as it relates to SAIs are illustrated in Figure 1.2.

Figure 1.2. **Key areas for supreme audit institutions to consider when assessing capacity**

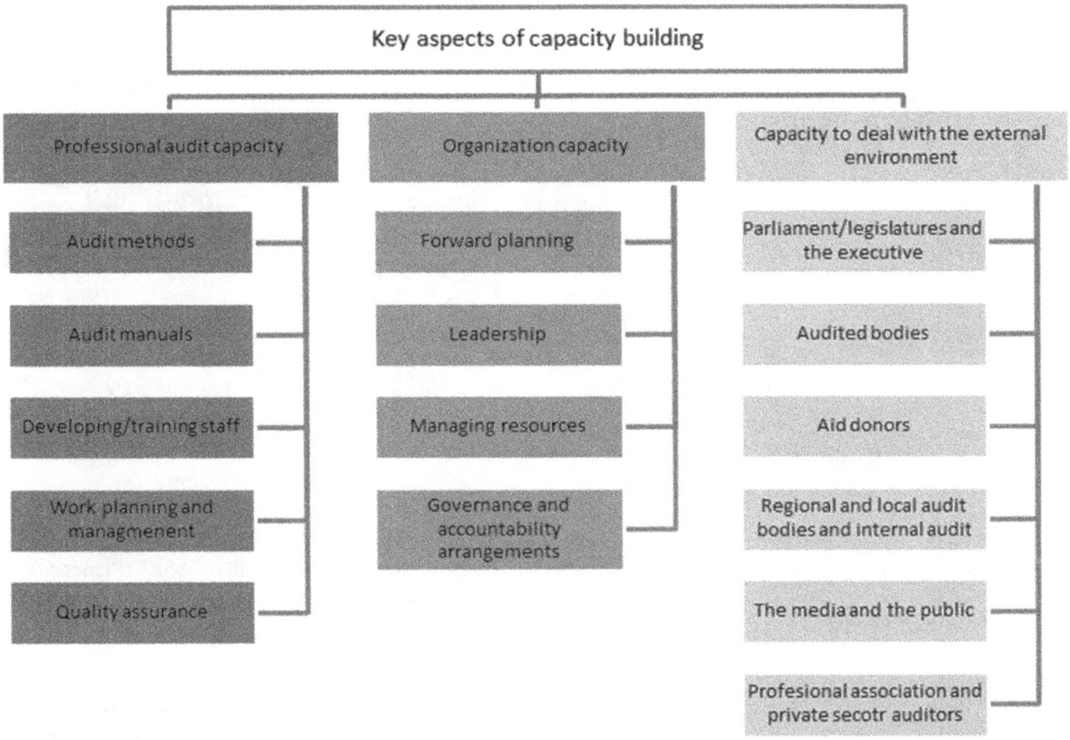

Source: INTOSAI (2007), "Building capacity in Supreme Audit Institutions: A Guide", INTOSAI Capacity Building Committee, www.intosaicbc.org/mdocs-posts/buildingcapacityinsaisguide_englishversion/.

ASF could adapt its risk-based audit programming to further prioritise how it allocates resources and reduce the volume of audits conducted.

ASF's strategic and operational agility, including its capacity to manage a high volume of audits, relies in part on the effectiveness of its audit programming, which it calls, the "Annual Programme of Audits for the Public Account" (Programa Anual de Auditorías para la Fiscalización Superior de la Cuenta Pública, or PAAF). The PAAF is ASF's methodological framework for identifying the audits it will conduct for the duration of one year. Figure 1.3 depicts the PAAF and its audit-programming processes. The methodology takes into account a number of factors, such as ASF's technical and managerial autonomy, the relative importance of audited entities, the variation in the amount allocated in relation to the previous public account, audit history, and complaint or requests from the Chamber of Deputies. It also involves consideration of available resources, types of audits to be conducted, and staff experience.

Figure 1.3. **ASF's Annual Programme of Audits for the Public Account (PAAF) framework**

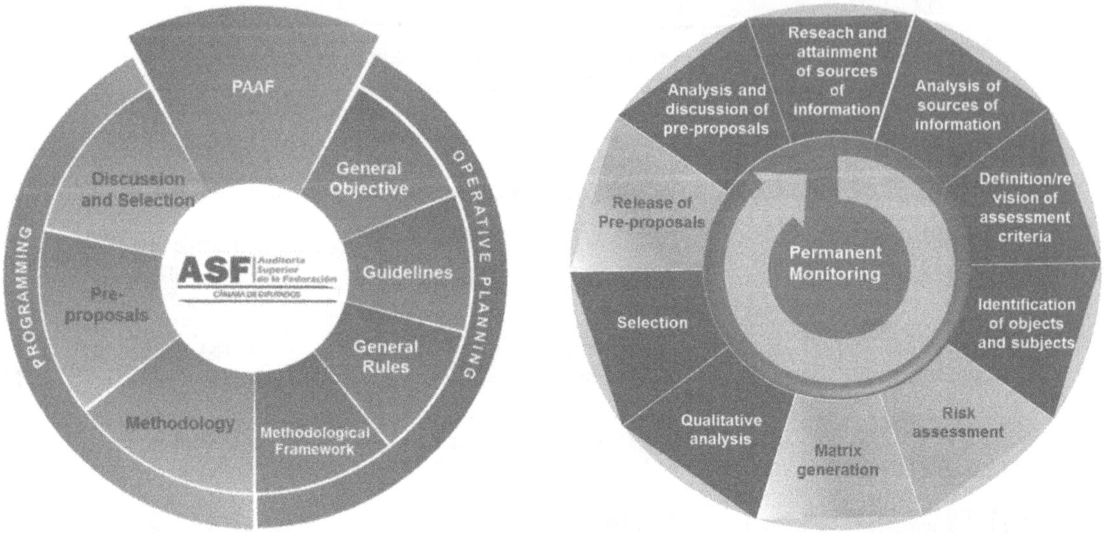

Source: ASF (2015b), "Planning and Programming of the Audit of the Public Account of ASF" (Planeación y Programación para la Fiscalización de la Cuenta Pública en la ASF), ASF presentation at the OECD fact-finding mission, October 2015.

Individual audit units in ASF propose audits or studies for inclusion in the programming process. The units have some flexibility to define their programming methodology according to the nature of their duties, but they must comply with the provisions of the overall methodological framework. As noted in Figure 1.3, the PAAF incorporates a risk assessment to identify and select audit priorities, which includes quantitative and qualitative methodologies for scoring risks based on 16 risk factors, and making risk-based comparisons to prioritise work.

Effective risk-based audit programming can be a useful approach for SAIs to direct audit resources to areas it deems to be most critical, based on a predetermined set of criteria. Risk-based audit programming can contribute not only to economical use of resources, but also to the evidence-based prioritisation of policy objectives and the effective use of tax revenue. Moreover, in addition to facilitating the selection of audits and allocation of resources, a risk-based approach to audit programming can aid SAIs in communicating its decision making internally and externally in order to ensure that salient issues are brought to the attention of managers and relevant stakeholders. Ultimately, this can strengthen the transparency of the audit institution and its justification for the actions it takes. Box 1.3 elaborates on risk-based audit programming in SAIs.

Box 1.3. Leveraging risk-based audit programming in supreme audit institutions for directing resources to the highest risks

The selection of supreme audit institutions' (SAIs') approach to audit programming will depend, in part, on their mandate and their level of discretionary authority and independence. Nonetheless, audit institutions can take different approaches to audit programming. One example is the "cycle-based" approach, whereby all entities in an audit universe (i.e. the range of organisations and activities that can be audited) are audited in year-based cycles, such as every three to five years. This approach ensures a total coverage of the audit universe within a certain timeframe, yet some audits may have limited or no value. Another approach is the "audit-on-demand" or "incident-based" audit programming. This approach involves responding to the demands or requests related to specific matters or incidents. For instance, in some countries, SAIs respond to specific requests of the Parliament, and they reserve resources for this purpose.

The "risk-based" approach focuses audit capacity and efforts on key risk areas of the audit universe. For SAIs facing an expanded audit mandate, like Mexico's SAI (the Auditoria Superior de la Federación, or ASF), a risk-based approach facilitates prioritisation of audits and targets resource allocation based on a qualitative or quantitative (or both) assessment of the audits' added value. This approach can be borne from necessity in a complex, resource-constrained environment, where it may not be realistic for SAIs to audit all entities, programmes or policies. Moreover, international standards for auditing call for SAIs to take a risk-based approach when selecting audits. For instance, International Standard for Supreme Audit Institutions (ISSAI) 300 on Fundamental Principles of Performance Auditing notes:

Auditors should select audit topics through the SAI's strategic planning process by analysing potential topics and conducting research to identify risks and problems…The topic selection process should aim to maximise the expected impact of the audit while taking account audit capacities (e.g. human resources and professional skills). Formal techniques to prepare the strategic planning process, such as risk analysis or problem assessments, can help structure the process but need to be complemented by professional judgement to avoid one-sided assessments. (INTOSAI, 2004)

Risk-based audit programming and planning in SAIs can vary, but it generally involves a process of criteria development, risk identification, analysis, scoring and mapping, prioritisation and selection of audits in relation to strategic objectives, capacity and resources. Criteria selection can be drawn from different sources, as illustrated in the examples below. For instance, criteria can change depending on different types of audits. For financial audits, material errors in the accounts of the programme can be a main criterion. For performance audits, criterion can focus more on elements of effectiveness, efficiency and economy, and the extent to which the policy or programme is achieving its goals. The risk map and result of the assessment provides an overview of risks, and the ranking reflects criteria linked to the perceived impact and probability of the risk, such as the length of time since the last audit or the occurrence of major changes in the audited entity. The following are examples from countries with risk-based audit programming.

Belgium

The Belgian Court of Accounts uses a "Financial Operational Risk Model" (FORM), which is an integrated risk-based planning model. The prioritisation of audits is based on three criteria, one of which is the financial-budgetary significance for evaluating the budgetary relevance of the institution on a consolidated level. Budget thresholds are determined and taken into account in the total federal budget. The second criterion relates to budget priorities and controls. As part of this, the Court considers policies as well as horizontal issues affecting different public entities. The third criterion involves general considerations based on the professional judgement of the Court's management. This criterion receives less weight for programmes with smaller budgets.

Box 1.3. **Leveraging risk-based audit programming in supreme audit institutions for directing resources to the highest risks** *(continued)*

Denmark

The *Rigsrevisionen,* the SAI of Denmark, uses a risk-based approach for audit planning. The analysis obtains insights into each department's situation and to uncover potential risk areas. Initially, *Rigsrevisionen* carries out a strategic analysis of each ministerial area and department. These analyses also include reviews of underlying agencies and public bodies as well as their management. Subsequently, a similar strategic analysis is carried out on in the public body. Further, before the audit is launched, *Rigsrevisionen* also discusses the strategic analysis with the management of the department and the relevant public body to avoid overlooking significant areas in the audit. The strategic analysis provides the basis for planning the audit, which is focused on the identified risk areas to ensure that required audits are carried out and audit opinions on the accounts can be issued.

European Court of Auditors (ECA)

The ECA has a yearly policy and risk review to take into account issues like developments in policy areas, stakeholders' priorities, results of recent audits, the work of other audit institutions and media coverage. This review helps ECA to define priorities and align them with strategic objectives. The priorities inform various audit chambers to prepare lists of proposed audit tasks and information on their relative priority. After consideration and approval of the tasks, ECA's annual work programme sets out the audit tasks to be implemented during the year and the resources allocated to them. The programme is reviewed and updated during the year to take into account any changes to priorities. In addition, performance and compliance audit topics are selected at the ECA's discretion on the basis of criteria such as risk of irregularities, poor performance, potential for improvement and public interest.

Source: Lonsdale, J. et al (2011), *Performance Auditing: Contributing to Accountability in Democratic Government*, Edward Elgar Publishing, Cheltenham, United Kingdom; Rigsrevisionen (Danish SAI) (2016), "The strategic analysis", 17 August, http://uk.rigsrevisionen.dk/how-we-audit/annual-audit/strategic-analysis/; European Court of Auditors (2015), "Work programme", www.eca.europa.eu/Lists/ECADocuments/WP2015/WP2015_EN.pdf; INTOSAI (2004), "ISSAI 300: Fundamental Principles of Performance Auditing", www.issai.org/media/69911/issai-300-english.pdf.

Documenting the assessment and the scoring of risk is important for communicating results and strategic decisions. Moreover, in decentralised entities where risks may be assessed among individual audit units, documenting the risk assessment process using common templates and methodologies is critical for aggregating and obtaining valid, reliable results. A lack of structure and processes to facilitate communication, particularly during the risk analysis, can result in incomplete risk maps, lack of ownership over the results and audits, as well as unclear definitions of the risks themselves.

ASF's PAAF, including the risk-based audit programming, provides the foundation for maintaining strategic and operational agility. However, ASF could review these processes in light of existing and newly mandated responsibilities, as well as an evolving institutional and policy environment in Mexico. Indeed, auditors that OECD interviewed expressed concern about the high volume of work ASF already conducts. Figure 1.4 demonstrates the high volume of audits ASF conducted prior to the implementation of reforms, with a nearly 70% increase in audits conducted from 2010 to 2014, while at the same time seeing a net decrease in the percentage of federal spending audited (as shown in Figure 1.5). This further illustrates a capacity issue relative to the number of auditors to ASF staff, which was approximately 2 000 auditors in 2014 in addition to 500 support staff (ASF, 2015b). The figure also illustrates an emphasis on, and expertise in, financial audits with both a performance and compliance focus.

Figure 1.4. **Total volume of ASF's audits shows gradual increase**

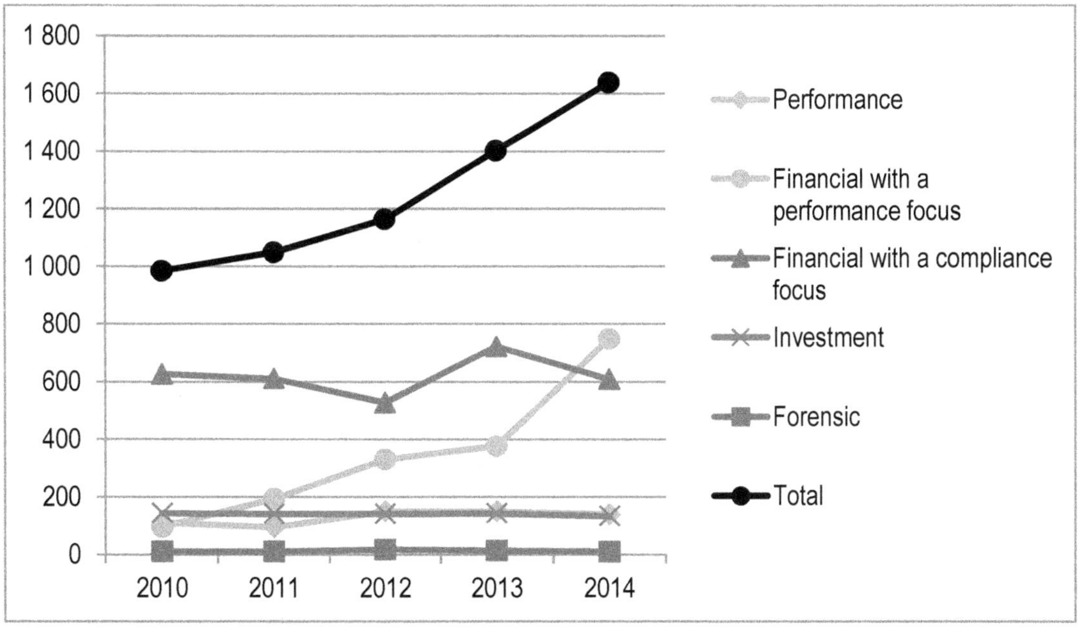

Note: The figure reflects ASF's core audit activities; however, a limited amount of ASF's work consists of studies and evaluations of public policies.

Source: ASF (2015b), "Panorama de la fiscalización en México", ASF Publishing, Mexico City, www3.diputados.gob.mx/camara/content/download/334211/1191134/file/Libro%20Panorama%20de%20la%20Fiscalizacion%20Superior%202015.pdf.

Figure 1.5. **ASF's audit coverage of federal spending shows a net decrease**

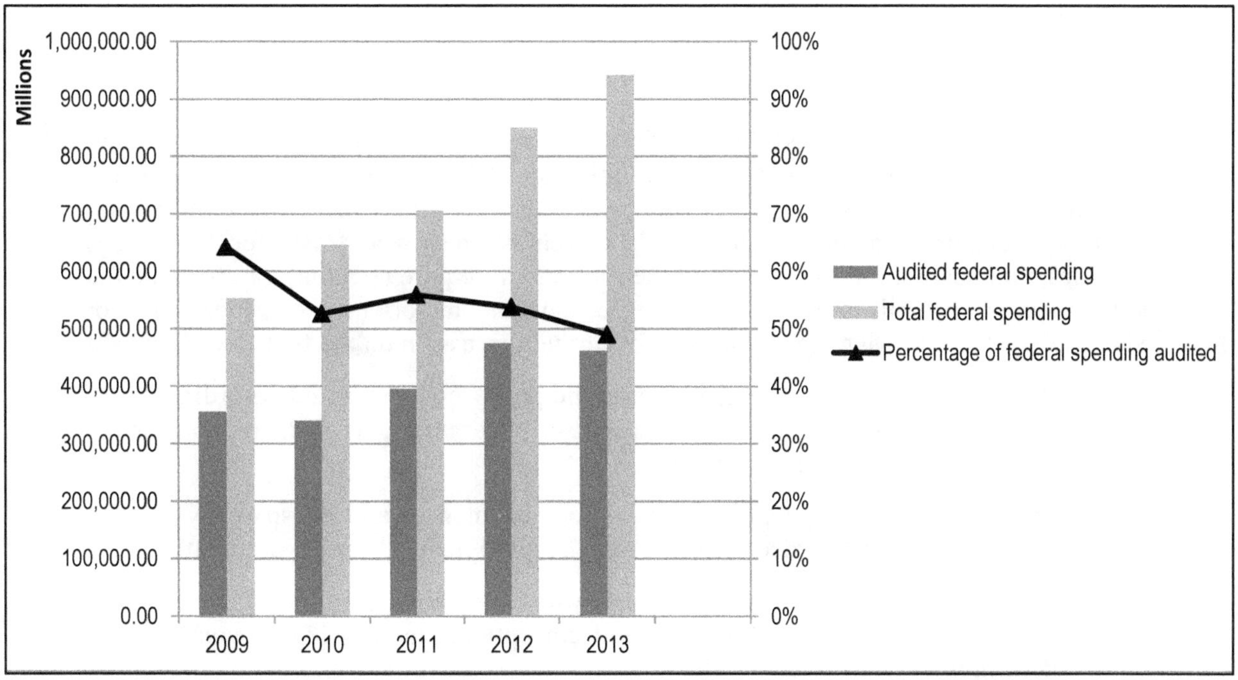

Source: ASF (2015b), "Panorama de la fiscalización en México", ASF Publishing, Mexico City, www3.diputados.gob.mx/camara/content/download/334211/1191134/file/Libro%20Panorama%20de%20la%20Fiscalizacion%20Superior%202015.pdf.

ASF risks overextension in the absence of a concerted effort to further define how it will internally manage its additional duties across the three systems, while meeting the demands of its existing portfolio. As discussed in this chapter, shaping its role based on its comparative advantage can help ASF to identify strategic areas where it could have the greatest impact and effectively use its limited resources. ASF could consider its comparative advantage through the lens of its risk-based audit programming with a view to maintaining the impact of its audit and agility. ASF could bear in mind the following when conducting the review (see Chapter 3 for additional discussion linking ASF's risk-based audit programming to specific authorities it will have as a result of recent reforms):

- Although ASF's risk-based approach to programming is robust, documented and allows for strategic prioritisation of resources, the high volume of audits ASF still conducts suggests the need for refinement of the process. Prioritisation of audits, effectively increasing the threshold of what is audited for a given year and reducing the volume of audits, could be a necessary trade-off in light of newly mandated responsibilities. Even in the absence of reforms, the current upwards trajectory of audits would be unsustainable without changes to strategy, programming, budget or resource allocation.
- ASF's current portfolio is heavily weighted toward financial audits, albeit some have a performance element. A review of the risk-based audit programming could include an assessment of existing criteria with regard to the diversity of ASF's portfolio and the types of audits it can conduct to provide a full picture of the effectiveness, efficiency and economy of government.
- Risk criteria that place a high value on the impact of performance or forensic audits, both of which represent a small portion of ASF's portfolio and have effectively remained as such over the last five years, could be considered during the review and potentially given more weight when revising the criteria.

Proposals for action

On a strategic level, the SNF faces various challenges to further define and implement its comparative advantage. To aid in doing this, the SNF could further define its short-, medium- and long-term strategic priorities and activities with a focus on its members' primary strengths in auditing. The SNF's current strategy and Basis for Operations provides a foundation for doing this, but the former will require updating for 2018 and the latter focuses primarily on outputs. Strategic and outcome-oriented considerations for SNF include the following (see Chapter 3 for further discussion on the first three bullets):

- Provide an overarching perspective on the policy coherence and co-ordination of integrity and transparency agendas across government, as well as institutional arrangements, to ensure outcomes.
- Ensure effective design and implementation of integrity and transparency policies through audits and related advisory work at multiple levels of government.
- Enhance integrity through reviews of systemic internal control deficiencies and support of investigations of fraud and corruption, emphasising prevention over detection.
- Model principles of accountability, integrity and transparency in the strategies and operations of SNF as a whole, as well as individual SNF members.

SNF members, as audit institutions, are responsible for promoting transparency in their external interactions and internal operations. For audit institutions, there is more to transparency than providing access to information, making it searchable or presenting it attractively, such as using plain language or creating simple web interfaces (OECD, 2014a). Specifically, transparency initiatives of audit institutions could consider a strategy that not only defines the what (right data), when (right time) and how (design) of the data, but also the monitoring and improvements to its actual use. **SNF members could dedicate an entity, such as a new Transparency Working Group, with the primary responsibility of co-ordinating with the National Transparency System and contributing to the effectiveness of the transparency agenda and open data initiatives.** Creation of the working group would help SNF members to be better models for transparency through a co-ordinated approach.

Defining and implementing comparative advantages can occur at the system level in SNF, as well as among its individual members. For ASF, this involves refining its strategy to effectively respond to an expanded mandate. **For instance, ASF could communicate a clear vision, objectives and procedures with regard to its forensic audit and new investigative functions that emphasise its comparative advantage in auditing.** Doing so will help to guide internal initiatives to develop its portfolio in these areas, and communicate its mandate and activities for conducting forensic audits and investigations to other SNF members and external stakeholders.

In addition, ensuring the effectiveness of ASF across systems calls for additional actions to meet new demands and effectively allocate resources. **To ensure its ability to effectively balance and respond to new responsibilities, ASF could conduct an in-depth review of key elements of its strategic and operational agility, including an assessment of its strategic sensitivity, resource flexibility and leadership unity.** These are key elements of strategic agility that can provide a framework for a deeper analysis on this issue, which was beyond the scope of this report. **Moreover, ASF could adapt its risk-based audit programming to further prioritise how it allocates resources and reduce the volume of audits conducted.** Although ASF's risk-based approach to programming is robust, documented and allows for strategic prioritisation of resources, the high volume of audits ASF still conducts suggests the need for refinement of the process. Chapter 3 explores ASF's risk-based audit programming in more detail with regard to new authorities.

Annex 1.A1

Transparency and citizen engagement in the state of Puebla

Audit institutions have critical oversight responsibilities over the public sector, and contribute to the policy cycle through activities that provide insight and foresight. They are critical actors to ensure safeguarding of taxpayer money and accountability of government to citizens. Engagement with citizens and other external stakeholders can strengthen audit institutions capacities and effectiveness in holding governments accountable, and mechanisms for engagement between audit institutions and external stakeholders have multiplied in the last years (Effective Institutions Platform, 2014). In particular, two kinds of engagements are salient: transparency mechanisms based on a one-way information flow (e.g. disclosure of institutional information and audit reports) and participatory mechanisms involving two-way flows of information (e.g. complaint mechanisms and the engagement of experts they need to involve a greater number and diversity of societal stakeholders in their design).

The State Audit Institution of Puebla (Auditoría Superior del Estado de Puebla, or ASEP) has put in place a number of initiatives that aim to promote transparency and increase the engagement of citizens in its auditing activities. The ASEP publishes its strategic plan from 2012 to 2019, which focuses on the effectiveness of four axes: auditing, anti-corruption, institutional development and relationships with institutions and citizens. In addition, the ASEP communicates information about its mandate, responsibilities and mission to a broader audience through initiatives, such as:

- A guide for citizens entitled, "What is the State Audit Institution of Puebla and what does it do?" ("Guía para la Ciudadanía: ¿Qué es y qué hace la Auditoría Puebla?"), which illustrates the role and activities of the ASEP.
- A graphic and report with the yearly results of auditing activities (*Informe de Resultados*).
- A biannual publication of a magazine called "Cuentas Claras: Revista de la Auditoría Superior del Estado de Puebla" that discusses ASEP's main initiatives as well as the work of the National Association of State Audit Institutions for external audit entities (Asociación Nacional de Organismos de Fiscalización Superior y Control Gubernamental, or ASOFIS). The first issue communicates to the public that auditing of common resources takes place in an organised, systematic and comprehensive way.

Regarding participatory mechanisms, the ASEP, like other state audit institutions, are undertaking some initiatives to engage citizens, including the following:

- a programme called "Poblanojitos 2", which aims to involve children in social auditing (*contraloría social*) in relation to a programme that grants tablets to pupils in the fifth grade

- interactive tools to introduce children to both auditing and the ASEP ("Auditoría para ninos")
- photo competitions on the values of accounting and on Puebla's culture ("Los Valores de la Rendición de Cuentas y la Cultura de Puebla"), which invites citizens to submit photos concerning independence, impartiality, objectivity, integrity, legality and confidentiality.

In addition, the ASEP website informs citizens about their possibilities to file complaints or allegations for misuse of public resources. This can also be done through a dedicated hotline ("Línea Directa de Atención Ciudadana"), or in person. The website also explains the eligibility, the procedures and the ASEP's obligations in relation to such complaints.

Source: Materials provided by the State Audit Institution of Puebla and www.auditoriapuebla.gob.mx/.

Notes

1. The Basis for Operations (Bases Operativas para el Funcionamiento del SNF) (ASF, 2015a), published on 22 July 2015, is the SNF's framework that aims to define the objectives, composition and structure of the SNF, as well as the duties of its members. See www.snf.org.mx/bases-operativas-para-el-funcionamiento-del-snf-1.aspx.
2. See www.asfdatos.gob.mx/ for ASF's online portal, the "Sistema Público de Consultas de Auditorías".
3. In general, strategic risks represent factors that affect an organisation's ability to execute its strategies and achieve its objectives. In government, these include risk exposures that can ultimately affect the ability of the organisation to fulfil its mandate and carry out its core functions and services for the public. Operational risk is uncertainty that results from inadequate or failed internal processes, people and systems, or from external events (Stewart, 2010).

References

Ackerman, John M. (2006), *Estructura Institucional para la Rendición de Cuentas: Lecciones Internacionales y Reformas Futuras*, Cultura de la Rendición de Cuentas, Auditoría Superior de la Federación, Mexico City, http://siare.clad.org/fulltext/2129400.pdf.

ASF (Auditoria Superior de la Federación) (2015a), "The Basis for Operations" [Bases Operativas para el Funcionamiento del SNF], published on 22 July 2015, www.snf.org.mx/bases-operativas-para-el-funcionamiento-del-snf-1.aspx.

ASF (2015b), "Planning and Programming of the Audit of the Public Account of ASF" [Planeación y Programación para la Fiscalización de la Cuenta Pública en la ASF], ASF presentation at the OECD fact-finding mission, October 2015.

ASF (2013), "Internal Regulations" [Reglamento Interior de la Auditoría Superior de la Federación], Article 16(23).

ASF (2011), *Plan Estratégico de la ASF (2011 – 2017)*, Auditoria Superior de la Federación, Mexico City, www.asf.gob.mx/uploads/58_/Plan_Estrategico_ASF_2011-2017_web.pdf.

Cejudo, G. M. (2012), "Evidence for change: The case of Subsidios al Campo in Mexico", *Study No. 6*, International Budget Partnership, www.internationalbudget.org/wp-content/uploads/LP-case-study-Fundar.pdf.

Effective Institutions Platform (2014), "Supreme Audit Institutions and Stakeholder Engagement Practices: A Stocktaking Report", www.effectiveinstitutions.org/media/Stocktake_Report_on_Supreme_Audit_Institutions_and_Citizen_Engagement_.pdf.

European Court of Auditors (2015), "Work Programme", www.eca.europa.eu/Lists/ECADocuments/WP2015/WP2015_EN.pdf.

Government of Mexico (2016a), "Ley General de Responsabilidades Administrativas" [General Law of Administrative Responsibilities], *Diario Oficial de la Federación*, 18 July, www.dof.gob.mx/nota_detalle.php?codigo=5391143&fecha=04/05/2015.

Government of Mexico (2016b), "Ley de Fiscalización y Rendición de Cuentas de la Federación" [Law on the Accountability and Submission of the Accounts of the Federation], *Diario Oficial de la Federación*, 18 July, www.diputados.gob.mx/LeyesBiblio/pdf/LFRCF.pdf.

Government of Mexico (2015), "Ley General de Transparencia y Acceso a la Información Pública" [General Law on Transparency and Access to Public Information], *Diario Oficial de la Federación*, 4 May 2015, www.dof.gob.mx/nota_detalle.php?codigo=5391143 &fecha=04/05/2015.

Government of Mexico (1917, last amended in 2015), "Constitution of the United Mexican States", Article 115, Pan American Union, Washington.

INTOSAI (International Organisation of Supreme Audit Institutions) (2010), *Principles for Transparency and Accountability*, INTOSAI Professional Standards Committee, Copenhagen, www.issai.org/media/12930/issai_20_e_.pdf.

INTOSAI (2007), "Building capacity in supreme audit institutions: A guide", INTOSAI Capacity Building Committee, www.intosaicbc.org/mdocs-posts/buildingcapacity insaisguide_englishversion/.

INTOSAI (2004), "ISSAI 300: Fundamental Principles of Performance Auditing", www.issai.org/media/69911/issai-300-english.pdf.

Lonsdale, J. et al. (2011), *Performance Auditing: Contributing to Accountability in Democratic Government*, Edward Elgar Publishing, Cheltenham, United Kingdom.

OECD (2016), *Supreme Audit Institutions and Good Governance: Oversight, Insight and Foresight*, OECD Publishing, Paris, http://dx.doi.org/10.1787/9789264263871-en.

OECD (2014a), "Rebooting public service delivery – How can open government data help to drive innovation?", www.oecd.org/gov/digital-government/rebooting-public-service-delivery.htm.

OECD (2014b), *Chile's Supreme Audit Institution: Enhancing Strategic Agility and Public Trust*, OECD Public Governance Reviews, OECD Publishing, Paris, http://dx.doi.org/10.1787/9789264207561-en.

OECD (2011), "International Workshop 'Strategic Agility for Strong Societies and Economies': Summary and issues for further debate'', unclassified document, OECD Public Governance Committee, www.oecd.org/officialdocuments/publicdisplaydocumentpdf/?cote=GOV/PGC/PGR(2012)1&docLanguage=En.

Rigsrevisionen (Danish SAI) (2016), "The strategic analysis", 17 August, http://uk.rigsrevisionen.dk/how-we-audit/annual-audit/strategic-analysis/.

Shkabatur, J. (2012), "Transparency with(out) accountability: Open government in the United States", *Yale Law & Policy Review*, 31(1), 79-140, www.jstor.org/stable/23735771.

SNF (Sistema Nacional de Fiscalización) (2015), "Información General del SNF", www.snf.org.mx/SharedFiles/Download.aspx?pageid=90&mid=121&fileid=264.

Stewart, F. (2010), "Pension Funds' Risk-Management Framework: Regulation and Supervisory Oversight", *OECD Working Papers on Insurance and Private Pensions*, No. 40, OECD Publishing, Paris, http://dx.doi.org/10.1787/5kmlcz7qq3zx-en.

Subsidios al Campo (n.d.), "About this project", webpage, http://subsidiosalcampo.org.mx/acerca-de/sobre-este-proyecto/ (accessed 31 May 2016).

Ubaldi, B. (2013), "Open government data: Towards empirical analysis of open government data initiatives", *OECD Working Papers on Public Governance*, No. 22, OECD Publishing, Paris, http://dx.doi.org/10.1787/5k46bj4f03s7-en.

UNAM (Universidad Nacional Autónoma de México) (2007), *La aproximación al Concepto de Autonomía Técnica y de Gestión de la Auditoría Superior de la Federación*, ASF Specialized Studies, Auditoría Superior de la Federación, Mexico City, www.asf.gob.mx/Publication/47_Estudios_especializados.

UNDG (United Nations Development Group) (2009), "Mainstreaming environmental sustainability in country analysis and the UNDAF: A guidance note for United Nations Country Teams and Implementing Partners", UNDG, New York, https://undg.org/wp-content/.../12/ES-Guidance-Note-Final-July-27.doc.

Chapter 2

National and sub-national dimensions of auditing in Mexico

This chapter draws on principles of multi-level governance to suggest ways that Mexico's National Auditing System (Sistema Nacional de Fiscalización, or SNF) can act on to close important legal, policy, resource and capacity gaps, and improve itself as a system of accountability actors. Responsibility for strengthening accountability, integrity and transparency in Mexico is shared between SNF and its members, and relies on mutual dependencies. In pursuit of these principles, the SNF and its stakeholders (e.g. the Mexican Congress) can draw on principles of effective multi-level governance that recognise the importance of co-ordination that is both "vertical" across different levels of government, as well as "horizontal" among relevant actors at the same level of government. To do this, as explored in this chapter, the SNF can take steps to close legal and policy gaps, strengthen its own formal and informal co-ordination mechanisms, address implementation challenges and improve the balance between centralised and decentralised approaches to auditing.

Introduction

In all OECD member and partner countries, there is a degree of decentralisation of competencies to line ministries and sub-national levels of government for policy design and delivery. Countries may forego a fully centralised public administration because of the benefits of sub-national devolution with regard to increased specialisation and allocative efficiency. However, the same decentralisation that creates efficiencies and more responsive policies can also create mutual dependencies between institutions. Mutual dependencies across and between levels of government logically arise when responsibilities for outcomes are shared and no single government entity can achieve results alone. These dependencies highlight the need for effective co-ordination and collaboration between institutions to ensure the achievement of shared goals and policy outcomes.

In the context of Mexico's National Auditing System (Sistema Nacional de Fiscalización, or SNF) and its members, the outcomes link to achieving the goals of accountability, integrity and transparency. To achieve these goals and address mutual dependencies, strong multi-level governance within SNF is needed, including effective co-ordination and collaboration. The governance is "multi-level" in that it relies on co-ordination that is both "vertical" across different levels of government (e.g. the supreme audit institution and state audit institutions), as well as "horizontal" among relevant actors at the same level of government (e.g. the supreme audit institution and internal control entities at the national level).[1] The SNF enjoys a pre-existing institutional architecture to strengthen co-ordination and collaboration; however, further efforts could be instituted to close "gaps" that can derail large-scale reforms and undermine the public's confidence in government (see Box 2.1 for an overview of types of gaps).

Box 2.1. Overcoming challenges or "gaps" of multi-level governance

Gaps result from the fact that levels of government depend on each other to design and deliver certain policies. However, in the context of Mexico, policies for promoting good multi-level governance must be balanced with the need to ensure that SNF reforms do not detract from the benefits of decentralisation. Indeed, respecting the advances and legal competencies of sub-national governments will also be essential, since there is no "one-size-fits-all" policy that can be applied in the same manner with equal success. Greater effectiveness and efficiency can be achieved where state and local leaders make decisions that are more responsive to their specific needs, and therefore, different priorities and means of implementation may need to be factored in. Nonetheless, when managing relations across and between levels of government, public entities are confronted with a series of challenges or "gaps" that can stem from mutual dependencies. These gaps can include the following:

- **Legal or policy gaps**: Such gaps result from incoherence between sub-national needs and national level initiatives. Neglecting to consider a sub-national logic can reduce the possibility for successful cross-sector policy development and implementation at the sub-national level. Additionally, these gaps can also occur when ministries take a purely vertical approach to policy issues that are inherently cross-sectoral (e.g. water, energy, youth, investment, etc.). If individual government entities apply their individual logic to cross-sectoral initiatives that affect or are implemented at the sub-national level, then the opportunity for "joined-up" or "whole-of-government" approaches is minimised. In Mexico, one can find a variety of legal and policy gaps across and between levels of government related to the SNF. Among these, at the federal level, internal control policies determined by the Executive and applied to line ministries differ from those promulgated by Mexico's supreme audit institution (SAI), the Auditoria

Box 2.1. **Overcoming challenges or "gaps" of multi-level governance** *(continued)*

Superior de la Federación (ASF) in accordance with international standards, and the legal frameworks governing states' SAIs can be found lacking also in terms of granting them the necessary independence to be effective in their oversight roles. Ultimately, a strong SNF could serve to facilitate the identification and sharing of leading practices within the country, promoting convergence around the standards and activities of top performers.

- **Information gaps**: Information gaps result from information asymmetries between institutions when designing, implementing, and delivering public policy. National and even sub-national strategies for achieving public policy objectives might face an information deficit if sub-national authorities and actors do not actively share their knowledge of what is happening "on the ground." Sub-national governments' views, however, are only "partial" – limited to their own area or territory. Thus, the national government plays an indispensable role in managing the information in such a way as to support a broader vision that can be linked to accomplishing public policy objectives. One major challenge for ASF, for example, will be carrying out new audit responsibilities (i.e. auditing additional "*participaciones*" funds in states) with, at times, limited information on the public finances of sub-national governments.
- **Capacity gaps**: Capacity gaps occur when there is a lack of human, knowledge (skill-based), operational or infrastructural resources. Capacity-development needs can vary with the pre-existing levels of public administration infrastructure. Long-standing sub-national governments with well-developed institutions may require little in terms of capacity building to assume new responsibilities. But, where sub-national governments or related institutions must be created or have a historically limited role, capacity-building needs will be greater. The capacity gap is not restricted to the sub-national level; however, it also applies to the national level in terms of managing multi-level relations, allocating responsibilities and funds, and ensuring co-ordinated, coherent policy approaches among central level actors. Levels of professionalisation of auditors at sub-national levels vary widely in Mexico, with traditionally lower capacities at municipal levels. Likewise, once approved, ASF will need to develop capacities in leading the SNF and in taking on a greater number of responsibilities.
- **Fiscal/financial gaps**: The existence of a fiscal gap between the revenues and required expenditures of sub-national governments results in financial dependence by the sub-national level on the national level. Thus, the sub-national level remains dependent on the national level for funding and for a fiscal capacity to meet its policy obligations. Meanwhile, the central government depends on the sub-national level to deliver more and increasingly costly public services and generate revenue. Falling oil prices are closing fiscal space in Mexico and the new initiatives call on governments to deliver change with the same (or even fewer) budgetary allocations. Strong multi-level governance helps leverage synergies and achieve economies of scale in order to generate savings without sacrificing performance. Reducing duplication, for example, is perhaps the best example of generating savings from the reforms that can be reused for other purposes (capacity building, for instance).
- **Administrative gaps**: An administrative gap arises when administrative borders and functional areas at the sub-national level do not correspond to one another. This is clearly evidenced in territories where there is an agglomeration effect arising from a set of municipalities that alone are much smaller than the metropolitan whole. Individually their influence may be limited, but as a group, they can be a strong player in the relationship among levels of government. The administrative gap is an excellent example of multi-level governance relationships based on horizontal mutual dependence, as this gap often generates the need for co-operation among sub-national governments. In Mexico, greater information-sharing and economies of scale may be attained from stronger horizontal co-operation between state and municipal audit institutions.

Source: Charbit, C. and M. Michalun (2009), "Mind the gaps: Managing mutual dependence in relations among levels of government", *OECD Working Papers on Public Governance*, No. 14, OECD Publishing, Paris, http://dx.doi.org/10.1787/221253707200.

The SNF aims to address some of the common challenges arising from mutual dependencies among audit institutions, thereby improving the national and sub-national "governance" of the audit institutions as a collective group. The SNF supports the effective implementation of audit policies across sectoral and administrative boundaries at federal, state and municipal levels in order to achieve governance in Mexico through strengthened accountability, integrity and transparency. For instance, the reforms are founded on the need for greater convergence, including the need to harmonise laws, as well as policies and practices across sectors (i.e. such as between internal and external control) and regions, by bringing lagging states and municipalities up to par with federal standards and best practice at sub-national level. This chapter draws on principles of multi-level governance to suggest ways the SNF can act to close important legal, policy, resource and capacity gaps, and improve itself as a system of accountability actors, as summarised in Table 2.1.

Table 2.1. **Proposals for action for Mexico's National Auditing System (SNF) to close important legal, policy, resource and capacity gaps**

Leveraging the SNF to close legal and policy gaps for improved auditing	The SNF could close legal and policy gaps to improve the independence of sub-national audit institutions in Mexico, building on momentum of recent actions to embody the SNF in the General Law for the National Anti-Corruption System.
	The SNF could advance a coherent, government-wide approach to internal control and risk management by harmonising existing frameworks and improving co-ordination between external and internal audit bodies.
	Over the medium to long-term, the SNF could simplify audit procedures for sub-national levels of government to minimise duplication and help ASF to effectively manage its expanded mandate to audit revenue-sharing transfers.
Addressing key barriers to implementation of SNF initiatives for greater accountability	The SNF could improve its governance structure to enhance its effectiveness, better align strategic objectives and address areas of need, particularly in municipalities.
	State legislatures and the SNF could increase budgetary resources and address capacity gaps to help state audit institutions fulfil their mandates and mitigate the risk of disparities across regions and levels of government.
	The SNF could strengthen the professional audit service and create sound human resource management policies in audit institutions that help to ensure independence and effective implementation of SNF initiatives.
	SNF members could address the "implementation gap" related to internal control and risk management activities by conducting audits and evaluations that encourage ownership, accountability and skill development among public sector managers responsible for these functions.

Leveraging the SNF to close legal and policy gaps for improved auditing

The SNF could close legal and policy gaps to improve the independence of sub-national audit institutions in Mexico, building on momentum of recent actions to embody the SNF in the General Law for the National Anti-Corruption System.

OECD member and partner countries use various mechanisms to improve co-ordination and communication across and between levels of government. These vary on a spectrum from very formal, like laws, to less formal mechanisms, such as meetings, working groups, and the use of information technology to exchange information. As discussed in Chapter 1, since 2010, the SNF existed as a voluntary co-ordination mechanism between internal and external audit institutions across levels of government. Members are bound, not by primary or secondary legislation, but rather by adhering to (signing) the founding SNF Agreement ("Bases Generales de Coordinacion del SNF" and "Bases Operativas para el Funcionamiento del SNF"). Additional instruments of similar quasi-legal status exist for the membership of internal control entities in the National Permanent Commission of State Controllers (Comisión Permanente de Contralores Estados-Federación, or CPCE-F) (that is, SFP at the federal level and controllers at the state level), who are bound by *Acuerdos de Colaboración*. In the case of external control entities, including ASF and state audit institutions, these agreements are commonly referred to as *Convenios*. However, despite these instruments, implementation of the SNF has been poor or entirely lacking among some members, which can be attributed in part to the lack of political commitment, as well as weak legal frameworks and binding mechanisms for compliance, which can represent a gap in both law and policy.

A legal framework for the SNF is critical given the governance context and the absence of compliance mechanisms in existing governing documents of the SNF. The Mexican public administration is characterised by a strong legalistic culture, and the lack of legislative backing for the system has the potential to limit adoption and the effectiveness of the SNF's strategic plan (SNF, 2015). Neither the initial agreement signed by SNF members ("Bases Operativas para el Funcionamiento del Sistema Nacional de Fiscalización") nor the bilateral agreements between the Superior Audit Office (Auditoría Superior de la Federación, or ASF), and members for specific activities (*Convenios*), while legal in nature, create disincentives or apply sanctions for non-compliance with the strategic plan. Moreover, in the absence of an authoritative legal backing, the risk of divergences between institutions within the SNF increases. More advanced members of SNF tend to lead and implement activities, leaving non-adopters even farther behind over time. In addition, the risk of divergences across political lines (i.e. states and municipalities of the current governing party being more likely to participate than others) is also a risk that stakeholders and experts raised in interviews with OECD officials.

Embodying the SNF into general legislation, relevant nationally, serves to strengthen buy-in among members and promote greater compliance with its strategic goals and action items. The General Law for the National Anti-Corruption System, which advances the earlier constitutional reform, is the umbrella law for the National Anti-Corruption System (Sistema Nacional Anticorrupción, or SNA). As such, it determines the governance of the SNA, including the creation of the governing body, the SNA Co-ordination Committee (SNACC) and the requirement that states create their own respective systems. See Box 2.2 for an explanation of Mexico's regulatory framework.

Box 2.2. Overview of Mexico's regulatory framework

The organisation and distribution of competencies in Mexico are determined by constitutional law, which defines Mexico as a federal state made up of 32 federal entities. These entities, in turn, have the municipality as the fundamental element of their organisation. The legal framework grants the federation, through the activities of Congress, attributions to regulate most economic, social, cultural, and political activities, leaving to the states the attribution to regulate household assets as well as a set of residual competencies, defined as those activities not granted specifically to the federal level.

Nevertheless, the distribution of legal attributions is more complex. There are in the Constitution up to 14 concurrent or overlapping attributions that allow states to participate jointly with the federation, including rule-making in activities such as education, health, public security, planning, urban regulation, environmental protection, civil defence, tourism, fisheries, culture, enforcement of labour laws with some exceptions, definition of municipal boundaries, and co-ordination with municipalities and other states.

In the case of municipalities, the Constitution explicitly defines their functions and powers. The Constitution allocates the municipality the powers and responsibilities related to the delivery of public services such as drinking water, sewage, treatment and disposal of wastewater, public lighting, urban cleaning, waste collection, transfer, treatment, and final disposal of waste, and commercial markets, among others. The Constitution also gives powers to municipalities to develop, adopt, and manage zoning and municipal urban development plans, authorise, control, and monitor land use, according to their attributions and inside their own territory, engage in the urban land-use regularisation process, and grant construction licenses and permits, among others.

The main sources of law in Mexico are: 1) the Constitution; 2) international treaties; 3) primary laws; and 4) secondary regulation. The Constitution prevails over all other provisions, and primary legislation and secondary regulation must be in accordance. National and State Congresses issue primary laws (derived from constitutional reforms) as well as secondary regulations. The Federal and State Executive branches enact bylaws (*Reglamentos)*, technical standards and circulars. Federal laws concern the federal jurisdiction as defined by the Constitution and States laws refer to the State jurisdiction.

In addition to this typology of legislation, further distinctions among laws exist in Mexico that depend on their scope or nature. Firstly, one may distinguish between general laws (*leyes generales*), which regulate general situations applicable to the overall population, and specialised laws (*leyes especiales*), dealing with a specific issue or category of subjects.

From a different perspective, one may also make a distinction between ordinary laws (*leyes ordinarias*), which are expression of the regular legislative activity of a Congress, and two other categories of laws: organic (*leyes orgánicas*) and regulatory (*ley reglamentaria*). The adoption of both the latter typologies of instruments is always provided for by the Constitution, which sets their scope and objectives. However, while organic laws specify the organisational and functional basis of government agencies (as per Article 90 of the Constitution on the organisation of the Federal Public Administration), regulatory laws develop, expand and detail the language of certain provisions of the Constitution in order to establish the legal bases for their effective implementation (e.g. Article 105 of the Constitution on the competences of the Supreme Court of Justice). Although the legislative process for both legal instruments is the same as ordinary laws, they play a particular role in the implementation of the Constitution, so in the hierarchy of norms they have an intermediate role between the Constitution and ordinary laws.

The same categories of laws exist at the state level, although not all States' constitutions explicitly mention all the typologies of instruments (e.g. the Constitution of Puebla, which does not mention regulatory laws although they exist in practice, such as the Puebla's Profession Law, or Ley de Profesiones para el Estado de Puebla).

Source: OECD (2014), *Regulatory Policy in Mexico: Towards a Whole-of-Government Perspective to Regulatory Improvement*, OECD Publishing, Paris, http://dx.doi.org/10.1787/9789264203389-en; Constitution of Mexico, Constitution of the State of Puebla; Mexico and its Legal System, www.llrx.com/mexicolegalsystem.htm.

The General Law for the National Anti-Corruption System now formalises the SNF in law, and has the potential to create an incentive for stakeholders to commit to collective responsibilities, even if legislation does not stipulate sanctions for members' non-compliance. Importantly, a national-level legislative mandate for the SNF helps to provide states with the legal hierarchy and reasoning to align federal and state laws concerning audit functions. Moreover, ASF and the Ministry of Public Administration (Secretaría de Función Pública, or SFP) are both members of the SNACC, and the SNF is formally linked to the SNA, giving it legal legitimacy under the Constitution, specifically Article 113, albeit vicariously through the SNACC. The SNF can be held accountable for results under the Technical Secretariat of the SNA. Any provisions concerning the SNF in the SNA can also outline the scope and mandate on the basis of which to form its strategic plan, with the view to hold the SNF accountable as a group for its results.

Formalising the SNF in the General Law for the National Anti-Corruption System presents several issues for stakeholders to consider. For instance, tying the SNF strictly to the SNA agenda, while affording it greater legal legitimacy, may frame all SNF issues in the context of corruption, with a proclivity towards SNF initiatives that focus on integrity and anti-corruption. Care should be taken to ensure that the strategic plan of the SNF does not lose sight of the value-added role of audit institutions in strengthening not just integrity, but also accountability, performance, and transparency (refer to Chapter 1 on comparative advantage). In addition, although the SNF is formalised in law, other legal and policy gaps remains, as described below.

In Mexico, the need to address legal and policy gaps to improve the independence of sub-national audit institutions is acute, and the SNF could address this as a priority issue. On 7 May 2008, a reform to Mexico's Constitution aimed to standardise some of the basic features of the Superior State Audit Entities (Entidades de Fiscalización Superior Estatales, or EFSEs), such as the principles for auditing and the appointment of leaders, as well as the mandate that they should have technical and managerial autonomy. Another reform, published in the Official Gazette (Diario Oficial de la Federación, or DOF) in May 2015, known as the Anticorruption Constitutional Reform, established the legal basis for the EFSEs and refers specifically to their autonomy:

> *State congresses will have state audit institutions, which will be bodies with technical and management autonomy to carry out their attributions and to take decisions about their internal organisation, functioning, and resolutions, as established in their laws. The audit function will be carried out according to principles of legality, impartiality, and reliability. Likewise, these bodies will audit the activities of states and municipalities regarding funds, local resources, and public debt. The audit reports of the state audit bodies will be public.*

Notwithstanding such reforms, a lack of independence continues to hinder the audit and monitoring role of EFSEs and internal control bodies in Mexico's Executive (*Contralorias*). The independence of external and internal audit bodies, underpinned by a legal and policy framework, is a prerequisite for these entities to effectively fulfil their mandates and perform their oversight duties. One of the main tasks for auditors is to hold governments accountable for the use of public resources, as well as for the results of their decisions and programmes. In order to ensure such accountability, audit institutions should have full discretion and a strong institutional mandate that protects their impartiality, objectivity and independence. This allows the audit function to actually influence the performance and behaviours of government institutions and public officials.

Principles of independence are fundamental aspects of both external and internal control standards, as discussed in Box 2.3.

Box 2.3. **International standards for ensuring independence of internal and external audit institutions**

Ensuring audit institutions are free from undue influence is essential to ensure the objectiveness and legitimacy of their work, and principles of independence are therefore embodied in the most fundamental standards concerning public sector audit. The International Organisation of Supreme Audit Institutions (INSOTAI), for example, has two fundamental declarations citing the importance of independence. Specifically the "Lima Declaration of Guidelines on Auditing Precepts" and the "Mexico Declaration on SAI Independence" draw attention to the importance of organisational, functional and administrative dimensions of independence.

- Organisational independence is closely related with the SAI leadership – i.e. the SAI head or members of collegial institutions – including security of tenure and legal immunity in the normal discharge of their duties.
- Functional independence requires that SAIs have a sufficiently broad mandate and full discretion in the discharge of their assignments, including sufficient access to information and powers of investigation. Functional independence also requires that SAIs have the freedom to plan audit work, to decide on the content and timing of audit reports and to publish and disseminate them.
- Administrative independence requires that SAIs be provided with appropriate human, material and monetary resources as well as the autonomy to use these resources as they see fit.

Independence is equally important for internal audit institutions. INTOSAI GOV 9100 – Guidelines for Internal Control Standards for the Public Sector and INTOSAI GOV 9120 – Internal Control: Providing a Foundation for Accountability in Government (which includes a checklist), both cite the importance of the independence of internal auditors from an organisation's management: "for an internal audit function to be effective, it is essential that the internal audit staff be independent from management, work in an unbiased, correct and honest way and that they report directly to the highest level of authority within the organisation. This allows the internal auditors to present unbiased opinions on their assessments of internal control and objectively present proposals aimed at correcting the revealed shortcomings."

More specific guidelines with respect to independence are provided in INTOSAI GOV 9140 – Internal Audit Independence in the Public Sector, which adopt principles from ISSAI 1610 (Using the Work of Internal Auditors) in defining independence. Criteria under both documents include: whether the internal audit institution is established by legislation or regulation; is accountable and reports directly to top management and has access to those charged with governance; is located organisationally outside the staff and management function and has segregated responsibilities from management; has clear and formally defined responsibilities; has adequate payment and grading, adequate freedom in developing audit plans; and is involved in the recruitment of its own audit staff.

Source: INTOSAI (1977), "Lima Declaration of Guidelines on Auditing Precepts", *International Standards of Supreme Audit Institutions* (ISSAI), 1, INTOSAI Professional Standard Committee Secretariat, Copenhagen, www.issai.org; INTOSAI (2007a), "Mexico Declaration on SAI Independence", *International Standards of Supreme Audit Institutions* (ISSAI), 11, INTOSAI Professional Standard Committee Secretariat, Copenhagen, www.issai.org; INTOSAI (2004), "GOV 9100 Guidelines for Internal Control Standards for the Public Sector", www.intosai.org/issai-executive-summaries/view/article/intosai-gov-9100-guidelinesfor-internal-control-standards-for-the-public-sector.html; INTOSAI (2010a), "Guidelines for Internal Control Standards for the Public Sector", www.issai.org/media/13329/intosai_gov_9100_e.pdf; INTOSAI (2010b), "Internal Audit Independence in the Public Sector", www.issai.org/media/13349/intosai_gov_9140_e_.pdf; INTOSAI (2001), "GOV 9120 Internal Control: Providing a Foundation for Accountability in Government", www.issai.org/media/13337/intosai_gov_9120_e.pdf.

Furthermore, a lack of independence also limits the ability of audit institutions to provide relevant, objective and evidence-based feedback to the policy decisions taken in state executive branches. An agile government calls for its governance actors to be receptive to relevant information that would lead to improved policy decisions and focused prioritisation. This can mean making use of principles, benchmarks, databases and findings developed by entities outside of the executive branch, such as audit institutions. Moreover, the external, birds-eye perspective of EFSEs can have numerous benefits across the policy cycle, such as helping to ensure the effectiveness and efficiency of government initiatives, and minimising fraud, waste and abuse.

Taking advantage of EFSEs work depends in part on the willingness of the legislative and executive branches to incorporate their findings into policy reforms or take sanctioning actions based on evidence EFSEs collects. Legislatures have the duty to balance the powers of the Executive and monitor the use of public resources. In this sense, state legislatures should make political and budgetary decisions, based on technical evidence and information provided by EFSEs. Likewise, state legislatures should ensure follow up on the work done by EFSEs. At the state level in Mexico, EFSEs have the power to identify potential misconduct or integrity violations based on audit findings that may suggest financial damage to the public treasury. However, some EFSEs cannot themselves execute administrative disciplinary proceedings, which are under the remit of Secretariats for Public Administration. In serious cases where a potential violation of the criminal code has been detected, EFSEs may communicate such instances to states' Attorneys Generals (AGs) who can determine whether to proceed with a criminal investigation. EFSEs audit work and documentation on irregularities can inform the AG's determination of criminal convictions.

Given this division of responsibilities, EFSEs rely on the AG for following through on its findings and observations related to potential criminal wrongdoing. In the event the AG fails to act in a timely manner on information provided by the EFSEs, the accountability chain can break down. The establishment of the Special Anticorruption Attorney under the new General Law on the National Anti-Corruption System (Fiscalía Especializada en Combate a la Corrupción), and its equivalent at the state level, could be an opportunity to address this issue and improve follow up on EFSEs findings related to potential criminal acts. In addition, standard procedures could be established on how state legislatures could use the audit reports presented to them to improve follow-up on the report's findings. Predetermined periods of time could also be given to audited entities to allow justification for observations and improve the timeliness and effectiveness of sanctions, when necessary.

There is broad international agreement that to be effective an audit institution needs to be independent of the government. For instance, as previously described, INTOSAI has declarations and standards that draw attention to the importance of organisational, functional and administrative dimensions of independence (INTOSAI, 2007b). However, the independence of audit institutions is often curtailed in critical ways. In Mexico, obstacles still remain in achieving harmonisation of legal and policy frameworks, and particularly ensuring these protect the independence of EFSEs and internal controllers. One of the main obstacles to the autonomy of these entities has been the subordination, in practice, of state legislatures to the governor's office. Governors wield significant political power in some Mexican states with few checks and balances imposed on them by the judiciary, the legislative branch, autonomous bodies, civil society or the press. This can lead to situations in which governors can influence institutions that require autonomy to fulfil their objectives, such as ombudsmen, freedom of information institutes and EFSEs.

Political independence of audit institutions is critical for their credibility and effectiveness, and therefore they should be shielded from political interference and capture. In addition, research suggests that the credibility of external control and the quality of financial governance, with regard to budget transparency, bureaucratic effectiveness and the control of corruption, are positively correlated (Santiso, 2007). In Mexico, as is the case in other countries, audit institutions face the challenge of having limited de facto independence from political actors. These actors can operate on different incentives and are subject to "two-level" accountability, meaning they are forced to account not only to the public, but also to their negotiation partners, such as other politicians (Papadopoulos, 2008).

Political capture of accountability and audit mechanisms can take different forms. In some states in Mexico, a political deadlock can be the cause of a lack of congressional approval to the final estimation of damages to the public accounts or launching of a sanctioning process. Political parties may also "negotiate" protection to their respective political officials in exchange for protection of those from other political parties. In addition, previous employment of the heads of EFSEs may also be indicative of conflicts of interest. In 2010, for instance, ten superior auditors had previously worked for the Ministry of Finance of the corresponding state government (IMCO and CUCEA, 2013). These threats to political independence can contaminate audit programming, the decision to undertake certain audits, and the objectivity of the findings of EFSEs.

The work of audit institutions, and how the information they provide is ultimately used, relies on the political incentives of legislators. Political incentives, which have a short-term horizon based on electoral cycles, are not always aligned with the long-term horizon of audit institutions that seek to achieve policy outcomes and improve governance. This misalignment can result in legislators failing to act on the findings of EFSEs work, such as failing to pursue sanctions against political officials implicated in wrongdoing. Moreover, governors or other higher level officials in some states may have supported legislators in their bids for office, thereby creating a "loyalty" link that prevents congressmen from holding them accountable. Such political incentives can be corrected by closing legal and policy gaps that exacerbate the risk of political capture, and subordinate the public interest to that of political parties or officials. Ultimately, the legal and policy framework should be such that political incentives lead to increased use of EFSEs work and greater motivation among legislators to follow up on findings.

The Mexican Institute for Competitiveness (IMCO) and the Centre for Economic and Administrative Sciences of the University of Guadalajara (CUCEA) found that lack of autonomy is a weakness among EFSEs in Mexico. Figure 2.1 shows that three-fourths of the federal states received a score of five or less (out of ten) (IMCO and CUCEA, 2013).[2] OECD's work with supreme audit institutions helps to illustrate one of the practical effects this lack of independence has on accountability. In a survey of ten leading SAIs, OECD explored ways in which SAIS are contributing to the policy cycle, including formulation, implementation and evaluation of policies and programmes. To effectively do so, the findings suggest that SAIs require autonomy and flexibility to engage across the policy cycle at their own discretion (OECD, 2016). Applying this to Mexico, external factors that limit the independence of EFSEs is likely to result in more narrow contributions to policies and programmes, and therefore limit the uptake of their work by the Executive.

Figure 2.1. **Study suggests need for greater autonomy among state audit institutions**

Scores on a scale of 1 (low) to 10 (high) on level of autonomy

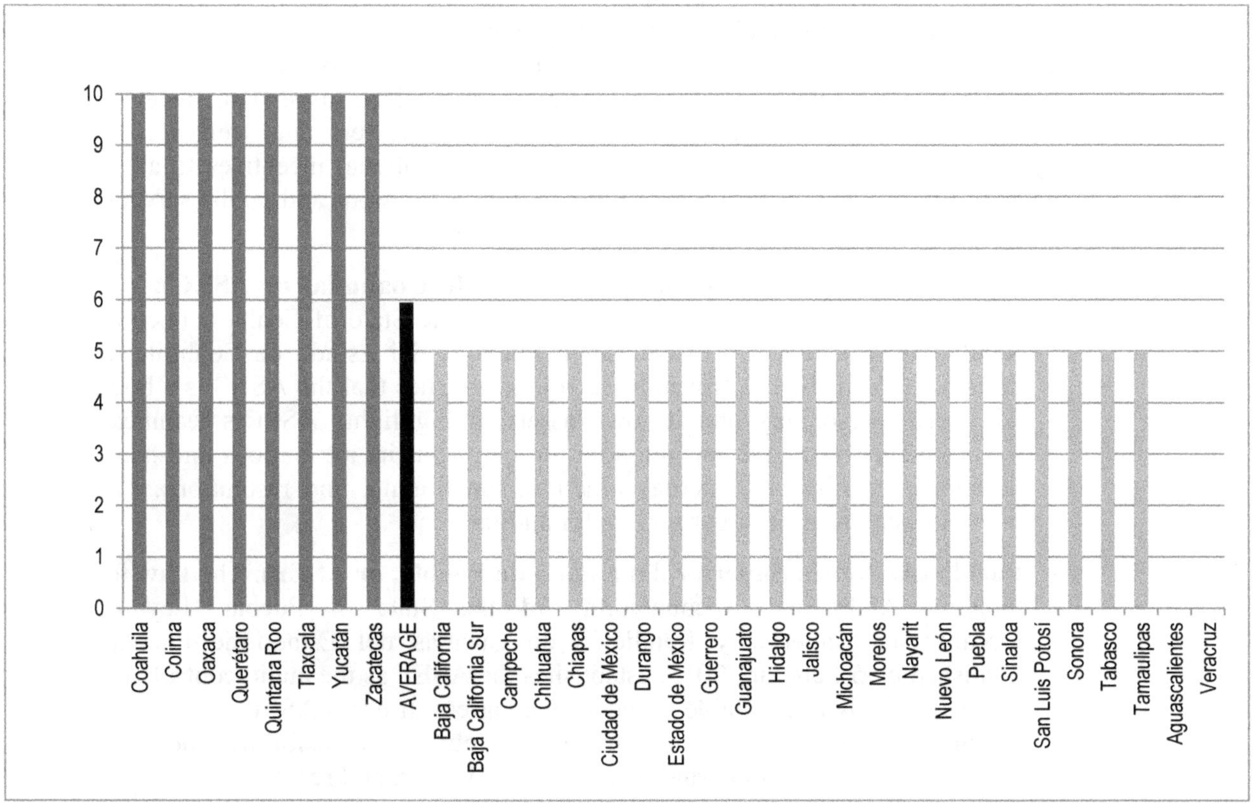

Source: IMCO and CUCEA (2013), "Auditorías Superiores Locales en México: Evaluación de su Normatividad, Prácticas y Transparencia", http://rendiciondecuentas.org.mx/wp-content/uploads/2013/05/Reporte_completo_IMCO-UDG.pdf (accessed 2 March 2016).

The results of the IMCO/CUCEA study confirm that the autonomy of EFSEs is often limited in practice, even if stipulated by law, because of the influence state congress or oversight commissions may have over them. For instance, in some states these stakeholders can approve the internal bylaws of the EFSE, make final decisions on damages to the public accounts, initiate procedures to allocate responsibilities on public officials and condition the publication of the annual report on the approval of public accounts. Other factors hindering the autonomy of some EFSEs are the absence of financial autonomy, the lack of specifications on reasons to terminate heads of EFSEs and the absence of a career service for auditors.

OECD's analysis of selected states, as well as the IMCO/CUCEA study, offered insights for practices that EFSEs could consider in order to strengthen their independence. The following are practices based on OECD's analysis and discussions with officials from the EFSEs of Coahuila, Puebla and Queretaro (see Annex 2.A2 for additional details about each state):

- **Grant EFSEs greater autonomy by reducing or eliminating the need for congressional approvals for internal decisions of EFSEs.** In many democratic systems, SAIs are generally accountable to legislatures, while still operating on the basic principles of independence, transparency, accountability, ethics and quality control (OECD, 2016). In some states, EFSEs require congressional approval for various internal decisions, such as the content of bylaws, determining damages on the public accounts or launching procedures to promote administrative and criminal responsibilities. For instance, the Law for Superior Audit of the State of Aguascalientes grants the Congressional Surveillance Commission (Comisión de Vigilancia) the power to modify, suspend or cancel the actions of the EFSE, upon justification. Such powers and reliance on congressional approval can create opportunities for political incentives to affect the audit process and the ability of ESFEs to hold institutions and public servants accountable. Additional examples include the following:

- **Coahuila (Auditoría Superior del Estado de Coahuila, or ASEC)**: The Law for Superior Audit and Accountability of the State of Coahuila (Ley de Rendición de Cuentas y Fiscalización Superior del Estado de Coahuila de Zaragoza), published in November 2014, establishes that the ASEC is a body with legal personality and its own assets. It highlights ASEC's technical, management and budgetary autonomy to carry out its attributions and make decisions regarding its internal structure, functioning, and resolutions. The law also establishes a career service for auditors.
- **Puebla (Auditoría Superior del Estado de Puebla, or ASEP)**: The Law for Superior Audit and Accountability of the State of Puebla (Ley de Fiscalización Superior y Rendición de Cuentas del Estado de Puebla), published on 5 February 2015, establishes the ASEP as the audit, control, and evaluation body accountable to the state congress. It notes ASEP should have technical and management autonomy to carry out its responsibilities and make decisions regarding its internal structure, functioning, and resolutions.
- **Querétaro (Entidad Superior de Fiscalización del Estado de Querétaro, or ESFEQ)**: The Law for Superior Audit and Accountability of the State of Querétaro (Ley de Fiscalización Superior y Rendición de Cuentas del Estado de Querétaro), published in December 2014, establishes that the EFSEQ is a constitutional autonomous body, with technical and management autonomy to make decisions regarding its internal structure, functioning, and resolutions.

- **Anchor the budget**. The budget allocation, subject to the approval of state legislatures, is an open flank from which political parties can attack and weaken EFSEs. As mentioned in the annex, in Puebla, the law establishes that the budget of the ASEP will not be inferior to the one allocated the previous year. This protection would allow EFSEs to audit and sanction without the fear of retaliation in the form of budget reductions by the legislature. Insufficient budgets may lead to staff rotation, lack of auditors, weaknesses in training programmes and other deficiencies. On average, EFSEs had a budget of MXN 121 million, according to ASF officials. Of the three states analysed in the annex, only Puebla had a bigger budget. Of course, the budget should be proportionate to the number of entities and the resources to be audited.
- **Make the annual report and other key documents public by default**. If the annual audit programme, the annual report, and the follow-up reports are not public by default, the window opens for the Executive Branch, political parties, and legislative groups to put pressure on the EFSE to reserve their contents. Also, legislators could delay the approval of the public accounts to avoid publication of

the audit reports. The Anticorruption Constitutional Reform already mandates that audit reports be publicly disclosed, but it does not explicitly mention when they should be published. In Coahuila, the state law mandates that the annual report should be published on the ASEC website on the same date it is submitted to Congress. This does not mean that audited entities will not have the chance to review and justify the observations received as this can be achieved by giving the follow-up reports the same publicity, so that anyone can see which observations were justified and which were not.

- **Create appointment procedures for superior auditors that are transparent, objective and merit-based.** In the three states reviewed, the election of the superior auditor, the head of the state audit institution, requires the vote of two-thirds of the state representatives. In Coahuila, for example, the appointment process is managed by the Commission of Finance and Public Accounts, while in Puebla it is managed by the Governing Board of the State Congress. In Puebla, the process starts by calling upon professional associations and boards to nominate candidates. This is a positive feature, but citizen representatives could also participate in the preliminary selection of three candidates. Instead of a legislative commission excluding citizen representatives, a more inclusive taskforce could be put together to make the proposal for Congress to vote. During the process, this taskforce could make transparent the assessments of their members on the different candidates, through standardised evaluation formats and exams. This more inclusive taskforce would also be a mechanism to avoid the process being captured by other political actors (i.e. the Executive). Citizen engagement should be pursued in the process.
- **Make removal reasons as explicit as possible.** Different degrees of clarity are found in the reasons for removal. Puebla's case, for example, is less explicit than those of Coahuila and Querétaro. For instance, the reasons for removal of the Superior Auditor of Puebla are detailed in the State Constitution and referred by the State Law for Superior Audit and Accountability. Such reasons apply as well for other public officials (i.e. the State Governor, State legislators, Magistrates of the State Superior Justice Tribunal), while in the case of Coahuila and Querétaro these reasons are specific for the superior auditors and they are detailed in the corresponding State Law for Superior Audit and Accountability. There is an opportunity for more standardisation in this regard to avoid state legislatures having discretion on the dismissal of superior auditors.
- **Develop a professional audit service.** The technical nature of the work by EFSEs calls for professional officials with the skills required to carry out sound audits. Moreover, EFSE officials need to be reassured that recruitment, promotion, development, and, if applicable, dismissal are based on technical and objective, not political or partisan, criteria. A professional audit service with clear human resource management policies would protect EFSE officials from political pressures. Coahuila's law requires the development of such professional service. See later in this chapter for further discussion.

Figure 2.2 summarises the practices above for strengthening the independence of ESFEs, and the potential effects of such practices.

Figure 2.2. **Practices for, and benefits from, improving the independence of EFSEs**

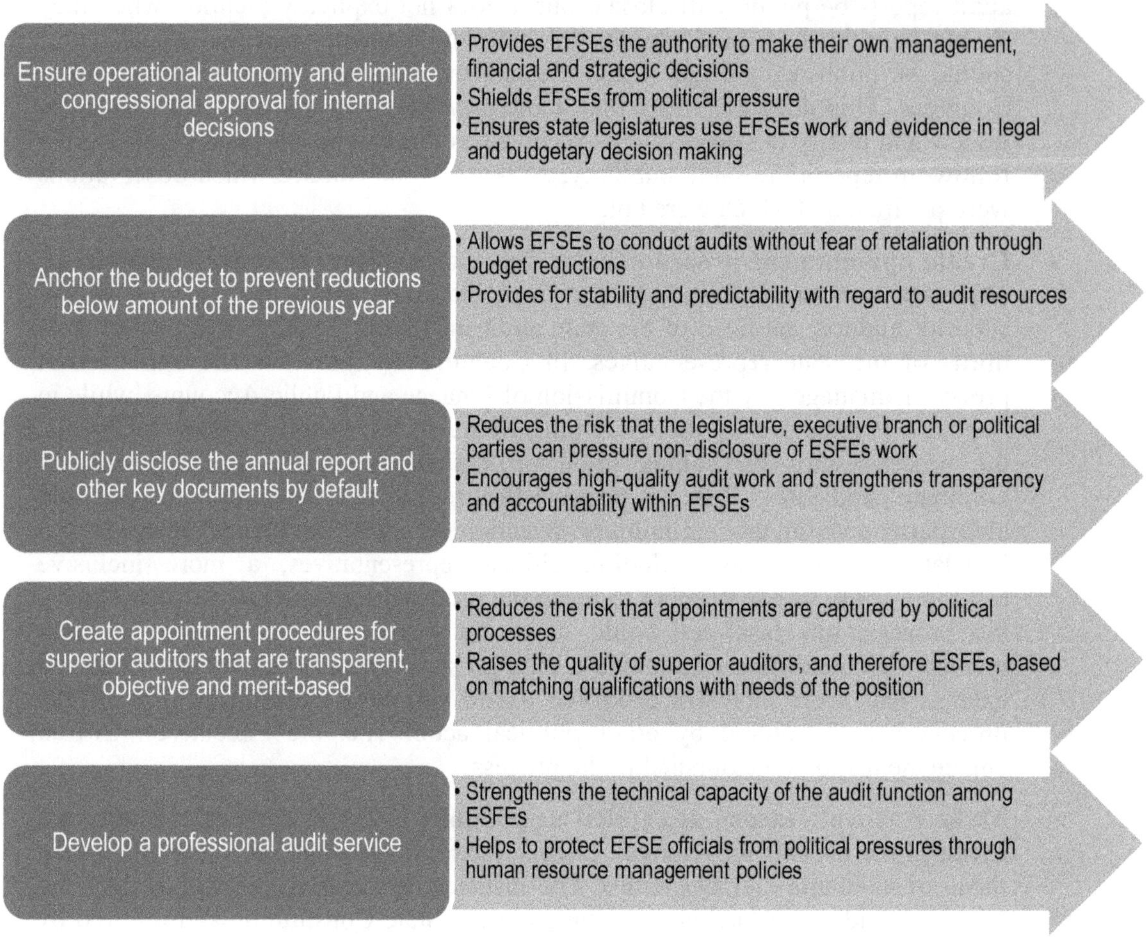

In addition to the EFSEs, internal auditors and comptrollers at state and municipal levels also face similar threats to independence. Comptrollers are appointed and can be removed at the governor's discretion (at state level) and the mayor (at the municipal level), and are therefore accountable to the heads of the sub-national executive branch. With regard to their administrative control function, such a hierarchy is reasonable. However, for the purpose of auditing related to potential corruption within the administration, political commitments may influence their independence to begin and carry through such work. One possible solution, discussed at the federal level, is to have the Senate appoint the comptroller (i.e. the Minister of Public Administration), so that the person is accountable to both the executive and legislative branches. States and municipalities could adopt a similar approach whereby state congresses and municipal boards (i.e. *cabildos*) have the opportunity to scrutinise the candidates for the position. Additionally, as will be discussed later in this report, a professional service of auditors may be created, with specific criteria to appoint the lead comptroller.

Audit institutions at the federal level in Mexico face fewer threats to independence, in part, because of stronger legal and policy frameworks. Harmonising legislation between the national and sub-national levels, under the auspices of the SNF, will help close the legal and policy gaps that threaten independence of state audit institutions. Additional legal and policy gaps to be addressed by the SNF exist in the areas of internal control and risk management (see the next section), and professional standards (addressed later in this chapter).

The SNF could advance a coherent, government-wide approach to internal control and risk management by harmonising existing frameworks and improving co-ordination between external and internal audit bodies.

One principal goal of the SNF is to improve and harmonise risk management, control and audit standards and criteria across the different branches and levels of government.[3] Priorities according to the SNF's strategy include aligning legislation, instituting common professional standards, applying leading practices in audit methodologies and adopting common frameworks for internal control and audit. However, divergences between frameworks used for these functions remain across institutions and, in some cases, gaps and fragmentation exist in terms of applying international good practice. These gaps and fragmentation have the potential to cause confusion among auditors and auditees, and leave government entities more vulnerable to fraud, waste and abuse. Central to this challenge are the different frameworks ASF and SFP use as criteria to conduct audits and monitor internal control and risk management arrangements within public organisations.

In 1992, INTOSAI conceived guidelines for internal control standards and updated them in 2004. These guidelines were meant to be a set of common standards for the design, implementation and evaluation of internal control. The updated guidelines draw from the framework of the Committee on Sponsoring Organisations of the Treadway Commission's (COSO's) for internal control and its enterprise risk management model to the public sector. Importantly, international standards for internal control highlight the role not just of internal control bodies, but also external control entities, such as supreme audit institutions. For instance, INTOSAI's 9100 Guidelines for Internal Control Standards for the Public Sector notes:

> *External parties also play an important role in the internal control process. They may contribute to achieving the organisation's objectives, or may provide information useful to affect internal control. However, they are not responsible for the design, implementation, proper functioning, maintenance or documentation of the organisation's internal control system. Supreme audit institutions encourage and support the establishment of effective internal control in the government. The assessment of internal control is essential to the SAI's compliance, financial and performance audits. They communicate their findings and recommendations to interested stakeholders.*

Moreover, INTOSAI's publication, "Guidance for Reporting on the Effectiveness of Internal Controls: SAI Experiences In Implementing and Evaluating Internal Controls," issued by the Internal Control Standards Sub-Committee, note that the role of internal auditors is critical for an organisation's internal control structure, but SAIs also play a key role. Specifically, SAIs are critical for: 1) establishing internal control standards; 2) creating a solid internal control framework; 3) working with internal auditors; and 4) evaluating internal controls as an integral part of both financial and performance audit. See Box 2.4 for an example of an SAI creating internal control standards.

Box 2.4. The Government Accountability Office's Green Book: A collaborative and consultative approach for creating internal control standards

The Federal Managers Financial Integrity Act (FMFIA) in the United States requires federal agency executives to periodically review and annually report on internal control systems. The FMFIA requires the Government Accountability Office (GAO), the federal government's supreme audit institution, to prescribe internal controls standards.

The "Standards for Internal Control in the Federal Government", coined the "Green Book", were first issued in 1983 and most recently revised in 2014, apply both programme and financial management. They are generally aligned with standards established by the Committee on Sponsoring Organisations of the Treadway Commission (COSO II) and set out management's responsibilities for developing and maintaining the internal control environment, risk assessment, control activities, information and communications, and monitoring. The standards are required for US federal government entities, the Green Book may also be adopted by state, local, and quasi-governmental entities, as well as not-for-profit organisations.

Though the GAO leads the standard-setting process for the Green Book, it adopts a collaborative and consultative approach. The Comptroller General established the Green Book Advisory Council (GBAC) in 2013 to provide input and recommendations for revisions to the Green Book. The GBAC consists of highly qualified individuals with complementary skills that provide a strong knowledge base in internal controls from entities such as:

- internal audit community
- federal, state, and local government
- academia
- organisations that perform financial, compliance, and performance auditing.

GBAC members serve two-year terms and may be reappointed by the Comptroller General. In addition to inputs from the GBAC, revisions also go through a public consultation and extensive exposure draft process. While the GAO has the legal mandate to establish standards, policies concerning its implementation are instead the mandate of the Office of Management and Budget (OMB). OMB Circular A-123 - Management's Responsibility for Internal Control - sets out requirements for conducting management's assessment of internal control over financial reporting. It is accompanied by an Implementation Guide to assist managers to comply with standards, assisting them with documenting, testing and assessing internal control effectiveness.

Source: Government Accountability Office (2014), "Standards for Internal Control in the Federal Government", www.gao.gov/products/GAO-14-704G; Office of Management and Budget (2009), "Management's Responsibility for Internal Control", Circular A-123, www.whitehouse.gov/sites/default/files/omb/assets/agencyinformation_circulars_pdf/a123_appendix_b.pdf.

Both ASF and the SFP have developed their own internal control and risk management standards and tools. In 2014, under the auspices of the SNF and the mandate of the Working Group on Internal Control, ASF developed the Integrated Framework for Internal Control in the Public Sector (Marco Integrado de Control Interno en el Sector Público, or MICI), which is based largely on the US GAO's Standards for Internal Control in the Federal Government. The SFP's internal control and risk management framework, the System of Institutional Internal Control (SCII), relies mainly on three models.[4] Within the framework of the SCII, the SFP developed a risk management tool (Administración de Riesgos Institucionales, or ARI) to accompany its internal control standards. Moreover, SFP also provides guidance and assistance to the Offices of Internal

Control (Órganos Internos de Control, or OICs), which have been actively involved in the process of developing a sound risk management and control system, as well as monitoring the implementation of the internal control framework in government entities.

Similarly, ASF developed the Automated System for Risk Management (Sistema Automatizado para la Administration de Riesgos, or SAAR), which is an electronic platform tool to aid practitioners to manage risks. It is accompanied by two practical implementation guides, including a Guide for the Self-Assessment of Integrity in the Public Sector and a Guide for the Self-Assessment of Risks in the Public Sector. ASF's approach emphasises the need for a risk management framework dedicated to fraud and corruption, in particular. Furthermore, it applies to all three branches of the government, unlike the SFP's framework, which only applies to the entities in the executive branch. Box 2.5 provides an example of risk management efforts at Mexican Petroleum (Petróleos Mexicanos, or PEMEX), a state-owned enterprise recently audited by ASF. This example further demonstrates the complexity of risk management in Mexico, as PEMEX developed its own model tailored to its specific context.

Box 2.5. A tailored model for risk management in the state-owned enterprise Mexican Petroleum (PEMEX)

Risk can be defined as uncertainty of the outcomes, whether positive or negative, of actions and events that will have an impact on the achievement of an entity's mission and objectives. Effective risk management requires, among other things, that entities identify and assess risks in terms of their likelihood impact, and then develop approaches to respond to risks and monitor risk-mitigation activities (United Kingdom's HM Treasury, The Orange Book-Management of Risk). An effective risk-management function can provide reasonable assurances that public entities will be able to meet their objectives. It can also help audit institutions to produce effective risk-based strategic and annual plans. A major challenge with public institutions stems from the quality and actual implementation of a risk-management system that goes beyond institutional "silos" and cascades through all levels of the organisation, including structural and operational arrangements.

In response to ASF's audit and recommendations from 2012, PEMEX developed its own model for internal control and risk management. As a result of the Energy Reform (2013), PEMEX was granted autonomy for its administration, organisation, management, and budget, as well as a new corporate structure. Article 2 of the PEMEX Law (Ley de PEMEX) established PEMEX as a state-productive enterprise, of the exclusive property of Mexico's Federal Government, but with its own assets as well as technical, operative, and management autonomy. This transformation triggered an ambitious ongoing project of reorganising internal control, risk management and internal audit functions. This includes an application of an Enterprise Risk Management Model (Marco de Administración de Riesgos Empresariales, or MARE) aligned with the company's competition and corporate governance risks and challenges. The figure below illustrates PEMEX's MARE and its relation to the internal control system.

PEMEX's MARE represents a third model for internal control and risk management, in addition to those developed by ASF and SFP. All three models share common characteristics, since they all draw from COSO's Internal Control-Integrated Framework. However, SFP's model is based on different internal control and risk-management frameworks than ASF's. All three frameworks and tools illustrate the high degree of sophistication and evolution of the internal control and risk-management functions in Mexico. At the same time, they demonstrate the duplication of effort and the lack of co-ordination into reaching a common approach towards harmonising the relevant standards and tools.

Box 2.5. A tailored model for risk management in the state-owned enterprise Mexican Petroleum (PEMEX) *(continued)*

PEMEX's MARE and its relation to the internal control system

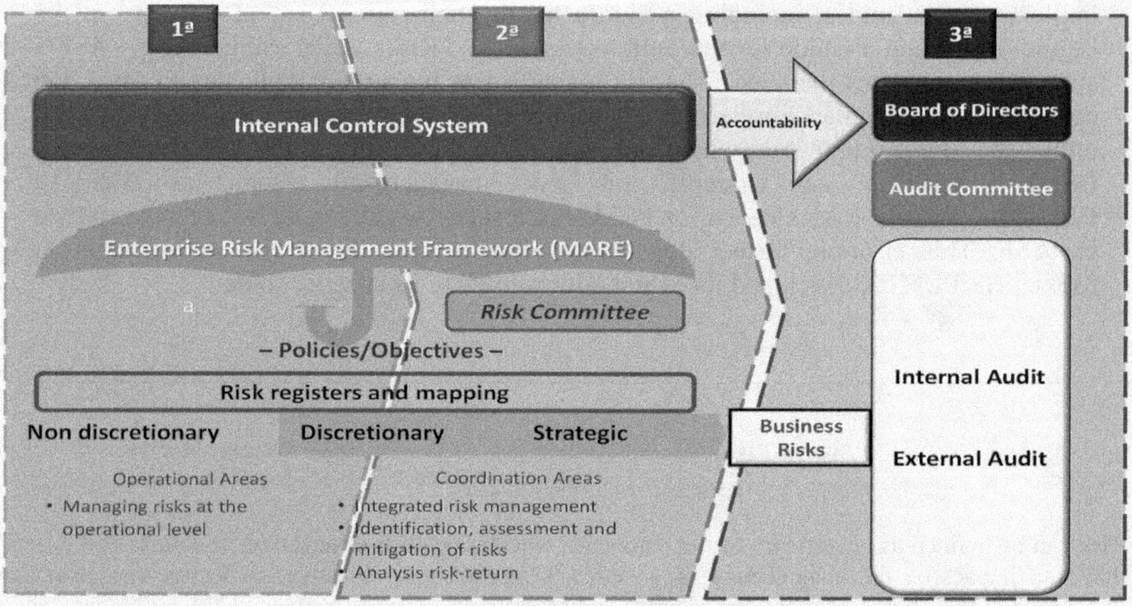

Source: PEMEX (2015), "Macro de Administracion de Riesgo Empresariales' Présentation", 25 November.

Source: PEMEX law and input provided by the Corporate Direction of Finance, Sub-direction of Risk Management, November 2015.

As illustrated Box 2.5, standards for both internal control and risk management are reflected in various models of both ASF and SFP, and in the case of PEMEX, an additional model (i.e. MARE) was also created. The models reflect the five critical elements of COSO's Internal Controls-Integrated Framework-environment: risk, control activities, communication, evaluation and continuous improvement; yet within these categories the individual criteria (or principles) vary somewhat from COSO's framework. Divergences in standards between ASF and the SFP are subsequently reflected at state and municipal levels, with differences arising in sub-national legislation, and auditees reporting frustration in the application of different criteria each year.

The fundamental concepts related to internal control and risk management may be similar across models, but overcoming the potential learning curve to understand the differences should not be the responsibility of the audited entity. Benefits of a harmonised framework include, but are not limited to:

- **Simplified capacity building and training of both auditors and the auditees, resulting in potential cost savings**. For instance, the cost for updating one set of standards and corresponding tools to align with evolving international updates and audit techniques would be significantly lower than doing so for two frameworks. ASF and SFP have invested significant human and financial resources into the development of their respective internal control and risk-management standards, processes and tools. They have also created training modules and certification programmes for managers and staff that are assigned roles and responsibilities in these areas.

- **Easier dissemination of audit-related expertise across all three branches and levels of government, thus improving effectiveness and efficiency**. The consistent application of frameworks and standards by audit entities allows for the effective and efficient application of internal control processes and risk-management practices by public entities, and the bridging of policy gaps related to the design of related processes and procedures.
- **Streamlined self-assessment and evaluation models**. Such an assessment would allow for more reliable and effective way of monitoring and measuring the actual implementation of internal control and risk-management activities. In addition, it would provide SNF valuable information on addressing core issues that hinder an optimal and highly functioning internal control system and risk-management function.

As discussed, international standards suggest a role for both ASF and SFP in developing internal control and risk-management models, and within the framework of the SNF, these institutions can co-ordinate to harmonise standards. The SNF's Working Group on Internal Controls could lead the effort. In interviews with OECD officials, representatives of government in the executive and audit institutions, at the federal and sub-national level, communicated the benefits of harmonising standards and processes on clarifying responsibilities, simplifying processes and ultimately improving integrity in government. At the state level, in particular, there exists a need to work both on harmonising the legal framework and improving relevant procedures and approaches for audit practitioners. Harmonising processes and tools across all levels of government can help to trigger a continuous improvement of the effectiveness and efficiency of internal control and risk management functions. The SNF provides a unique opportunity to mainstream all these standards and tools as well as training modules into one single approach. Doing so would not only benefit ASF, the SFP and internal control bodies, but also the public entities across levels and branches of government that manage or audit internal control and risk management efforts as part of their day-to-day work.

Improved co-operation between ASF and SFP relies on a number of factors, first and foremost being a commitment to take an active role and willingness to make necessary changes. Both INTOSAI and the Institute of Internal Auditors (IIA) have issued international standards and guidance relating to the co-ordination and co-operation between SAIs and internal auditors in the public sector, including: INTOSAI GOV 9150 "Co-ordination and Co-operation between SAIs and Internal Auditors in the Public Sector" (2010); and IIA Standard 2050 and Practice Advisory 2050-1-2-3 "Co-ordination" (2013). Moreover, a recent paper prepared jointly by the European Organisation of Supreme Audit Institutions (EUROSAI) and the European Confederation of Institutes of Internal Auditing (ECIIA), helps to elaborate on the main trends on the co-ordination between external and internal audit institutions (see Box 2.6).

Box 2.6. Joint study shows benefits and best practices for better co-ordination and co-operation between external and internal control entities

In 2014, EUROSAI-ECIIA published a study that elaborated on mechanisms and challenges for co-operation and co-ordination between external and internal audit entities. The following are some of the key findings from the report:

1. A very large majority of SAIs state using international standards or international references regarding co-ordination and co-operation with internal audit institutions. Most of them refer in general to the International Standards for Supreme Audit Institutions (ISSAIs), International Standards on Auditing (ISAs) and INTOSAI's GOV standards, such as ISSAI 1610, ISA 610, INTOSAI GOV 9140 and INTOSAI GOV 9150. Only a minority have explicit, written SAI internal rules, such as auditing manuals, standards, guidance, procedures or checklists, documenting and formalising the co-ordination and co-operation channels.
2. Co-ordination and co-operation between SAIs and internal auditors is often described as "informal," which can be difficult to assess or ensure the quality of its implementation.
3. The most common benefits of co-operation and co-ordination cited include:
   - Promoting good governance by exchange of ideas and knowledge.
   - More effective and efficient audits based on a clearer understanding of respective audit roles with better co-ordinated internal and external audit activity resulting from co-ordinated planning and communication.
   - Refined audit scope for SAIs and internal auditors. However, almost half of the responding SAIs state they experience risks or see potential risks from co-ordination co-operation.
4. A majority of SAIs pursued co-ordination and co-operation largely in the following areas:
   - evaluating the audited entity's internal control framework and risk management
   - evaluating the entity's compliance with laws and regulations
   - documenting the entity's systems and operational processes.

Source: EUROSAI-ECIIA (2014), "Co-ordination and Co-operation between Supreme Audit Institutions and Internal Auditors in the Public Sector", joint paper, www.eciia.eu/wp-content/uploads/2014/05/EUROSAI_ECIIA_Joint_Paper_05052014.pdf.

As indicated in Box 2.6, external auditors may perceive risks related to co-operation and co-ordination with internal control bodies. Moreover, from the perspective of internal control bodies, this relationship can become difficult if the external auditor is seen as the supervisor or assessor of the internal auditor. It is not uncommon for the external auditor to identify the opportunity for improvement in the work of the internal auditor when undertaking the task to assess his work. For instance, in the Mexican context, one of the main tasks of the SNF's Working Group on Internal Control is to ensure the process for effective auditing of the Offices of Internal Control (OIC). Moreover, ASF issued, in 2013, a study (study number 1172) on the actual implementation and the maturity of the internal control components within the federal entities, with a follow-up study the next year. This is an example of an external audit institution, like ASF, that has the task to assess and provide assurance over the effectiveness of the internal control and audit processes and activities. The challenge for external and internal audit institutions is to recognise the potential cost savings and benefits to improved performance through fruitful exchanges of views, experiences and expertise, regardless of other professional engagements the entities may have.

The experience of other countries provides insights on building effective relationships between external and internal audit entities, as well as mutual benefits. In some countries these relations are formal and laid down in laws and regulations; however, some countries, like Germany and Sweden, do not have legal frameworks or formal agreements that outline the rules for co-operation and exchange of information between the internal and external control functions. In Germany, for instance, apart from a few exceptions, internal audit services were only set up in federal departments and agencies in the late 1990s. Since then, relations between the SAI and internal audit services focused on the establishing of such services and on capacity-building issues. There is no general policy of or obligation for the SAI to evaluate whether internal audit was carried out with due professional care. In Sweden, the internal audit team submits its audit plan and its reports to the Swedish National Audit Office for information (European Union, 2012 and 2014). Box 2.7 provides additional country examples.

Box 2.7. Countries illustrate various approaches to co-ordination between external and internal audit bodies

Supreme audit institutions (SAIs) and internal control bodies co-ordinate in a variety of ways, as illustrated in the examples below. In some countries, co-ordination between the external and internal control entities is described in legislation or standards, which can mandate that the heads of these entities take action to share information, communicate and advise one another on audit activities. Informal relationships can also exist, where external and internal audit entities collaborate on an ad hoc basis based on professional relationships in the pursuit of shared objectives. The following are select examples from countries on such collaboration.

Australia

According to Australian National Audit Office (ANAO), professional standards encourage co-operation between internal and external audit to increase audit efficiency by minimising duplication. There can be mutual benefits for the auditees and the external auditor, in the case where internal audit conducts work that can be relied on by the external auditor, particularly in the areas of legal compliance and financial system controls.

Belgium

In the Flemish Community of Belgium the benefits are realised and maximised through consultation between the supreme audit institution and internal audit about: the results of monitoring and risk analysis; the consultation about planning (which audit topics overlap, timing and spread of the topics); the participation of the SAI and internal audit to management boards and management committees; the organisation of and active participation in workshops and information sessions; the systematic exchange of reports and manuals; and the review by the SAI of internal audit's internal control guide.

Poland

Co-operation between Poland's SAI, the Supreme Audit Office (NIK), and internal audit functions is required both in laws and standards for internal control, including Poland's Internal Audit Standards in the Public Finance Sector Entities. Reports of the internal audit entity are shared with the NIK, and the internal and external control entities communicate in the event of potential corruption, fraud or wrongdoing. In addition, the head of the Internal Audit Unit is tasked with minimising duplication between the activities of audit entities, and assesses the costs and effectiveness of co-ordination with the NIK.

Box 2.7. **Countries illustrate various approaches to co-ordination between external and internal audit bodies** ***(continued)***

United Kingdom

In central government, the National Audit Office (NAO), under the Comptroller and Auditor General, is responsible for external audit. The NAO audits the financial statements of all central government departments, agencies and other public bodies and reports the results to Parliament. It also carries out approximately 60 value-for-money studies each year looking at how government projects, programmes and initiatives have been implemented. Internal audit and external audit are encouraged to co-operate by sharing strategies, plans and working practices to optimise audit coverage and reduce the audit burden on the organisation. External auditors may seek to place reliance on internal audit work in accordance with ISA 610 if it considers that the work is sufficiently objective and technically competent and has been carried out with due professional care.

Source: European Union (2014), "Compendium of the public internal control systems in the EU Member States", http://ec.europa.eu/budget/pic/lib/book/compendium/HTML/index.html; ANAO (2012), "Public Sector Internal Audit", Better Practice Guide, September, www.anao.gov.au/sites/g/files/net616/f/2012_Public_Sector_Internal_Audit.pdf; EUROSAI-ECIIA (2014), "Co-ordination and Co-operation between Supreme Audit Institutions and Internal Auditors in the Public Sector", joint paper, www.eciia.eu/wp-content/uploads/2014/05/EUROSAI_ECIIA_Joint_Paper_05052014.pdf.

SNF's strategic plan and agreements between stakeholders, as described in Chapters 1 and 3, provide an important foundation for co-operation and exchange of information between ASF and SFP, as well as other SNF members. Going beyond co-operation to harmonise criteria, ASF and SFP could further explore constructive means for co-ordination, keeping in mind the following considerations that draw from international practices:

- Internal audit bodies can provide information, audit plans and reports to the SAI, and vice versa, for conducting audits, including evaluations of the effectiveness of internal control and risk management.
- Audit organisations co-operating on methodological and training matters can leverage economies of scale.
- SAIs can act as an advisor or observer, and take part in regular meetings of the heads responsible for internal audit (such as the case in Austria, Bulgaria, Denmark, Hungary, Latvia, Netherlands, Poland and United Kingdom).
- Audit committees or equivalent bodies in public entities can streamline the interaction and the communication with both external and internal audit bodies.
- Common standards, tools and procedures can facilitate effective co-operation and should ideally be agreed on by both parties, documented and approved by the SNF, as discussed in Chapter 1 with regard to harmonisation of standards.

Under the auspices of the SNF, internal and external auditors already co-operate in a variety of ways, including some mentioned above. To improve this co-operation, it is essential that the external and internal auditors communicate early and on a structured approach to help eliminate duplicate work, avoid surprises, gain efficiencies and enhance audit quality. Additional guidance could consolidate on actual experiences of effective co-operation and identify opportunities and concrete actions to help maximise the benefits to be gained for all involved parties across the three branches and all levels of government.

Over the medium to long term, the SNF could simplify audit procedures for sub-national levels of government to minimise duplication and help ASF to effectively manage its expanded mandate to audit revenue-sharing transfers.

Recent reforms will result in a potential expansion of ASF's audit universe to include revenue-sharing transfers to states (i.e. *participaciones*). Specifically, reforms to the General Law on Auditing and Accountability (Ley General de Fiscalización y Rendición de Cuentas de la Federación), the Law on Fiscal Co-ordination (Ley de Coordinación Fiscal), and the Law on Government Accounting (Ley General de Contabilidad Gubernamental) permit ASF to conduct audits on the use of these funds, an authority it did not previously have. Revenue-sharing transfers are granted as compensation for states' contributions to the national economy. They are non-earmarked and formula-based, consisting of a set of seven funds that vary in size and are itemised in the line-item of the federal budget, along with transfers to compensate states for collecting federal taxes (i.e. *incentivos*) (OECD, 2013). Both non-earmarked transfers (*participaciones*) and earmarked transfers (*aportaciones*) together account for about 80% of total federal transfers (or 27% of the total federal budget). The addition of *participaciones* funds to ASF's mandate increased the institution's potential auditing universe, in monetary terms, by approximately 16%. Figure 2.3 illustrates this increase as a result of ASF's expanded audit authority to include not only federal spending, but also non-earmarked federal transfers to states.

Figure 2.3. **Federal transfers to states show potential expansion of ASF's audit universe**

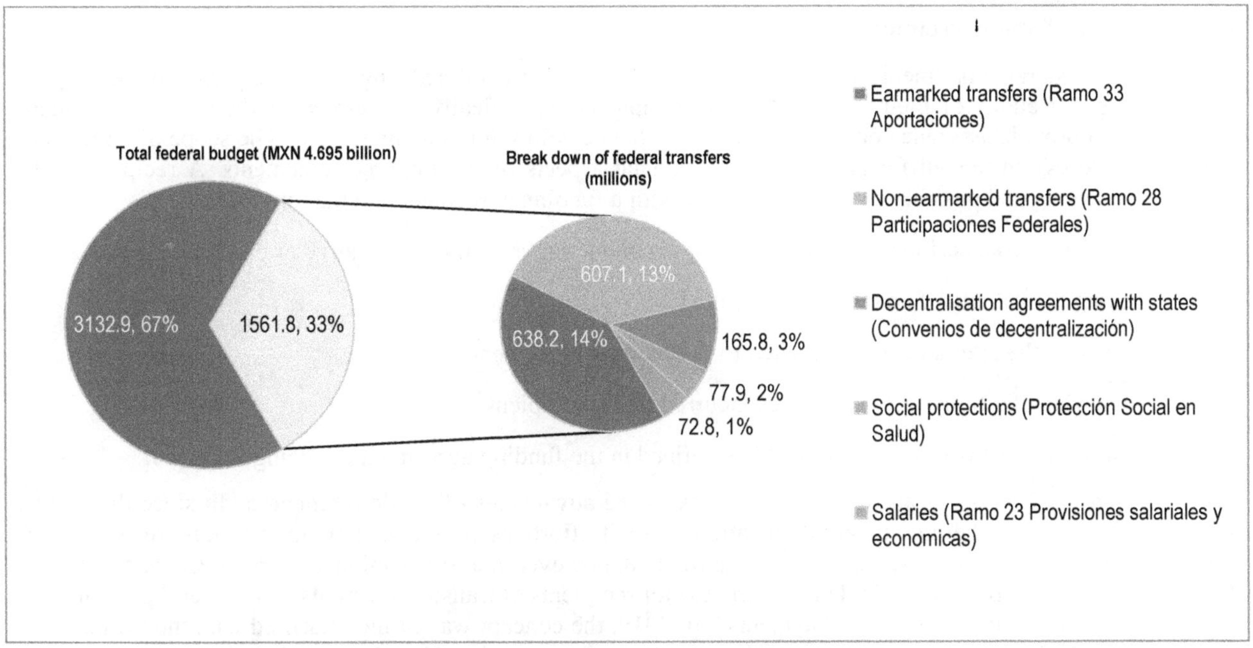

Source: Adapted from Centre for Public Finances of the Mexican Chamber of Deputies (2015), "Informative Note on Subnational Spending", January, www.cefp.gob.mx/publicaciones/nota/2015/enero/notacefp0032015.pdf (accessed 7 July 2016).

ASF's increased mandate adds to the complexity of audits within the SNF itself. In interviews with OECD, stakeholders from sub-national governments expressed concerns over the risk of duplication and fragmentation, a challenge compounded further by the application of different auditing criteria and standards. It also adds considerably to the workload of audit institutions that may not receive corresponding increases in additional resources and capacities to meet this obligation. In 2014, according to ASF data, it conducted 1 173 audits of federal transfers (*gasto federalizado*), covering only about 51% of the auditing universe at the time, excluding revenue-sharing transfers. Of these, just over half were conducted by state audit institutions through co-ordinated audits. The expansion of the audit universe to cover revenue-sharing transfers adds a considerable responsibility and potential burden to audit institutions.

Therefore, to fulfil the obligations that come with the expanded mandate, avoid duplication and minimise audit fatigue of internal and external auditors in the oversight of federal transfers, the SNF could consider closing legal and policy gaps over the medium and long term. This could include adopting laws and policies similar to those of other countries (see Box 2.8) that are commonly referred to as "single audit" approaches. A single audit aims to streamline oversight through simplification of audit methodologies and adjusting audit requirements of eligible government entities to predetermined budgetary thresholds. Canada, the United Kingdom and the United States are among the countries that undertake this project.

Box 2.8. Reducing duplication and audit burden across levels of government

Canada's use of single recipient audits

Canadian federal departments are encouraged to use a more streamlined single audit approach in developing and carrying out audits of their contributions to recipients. Specifically, a recipient audit is an independent assessment to provide assurance on a recipient's compliance with a funding agreement. The scope of a recipient audit may address any or all financial and non-financial aspects of the funding agreements. A recipient audit involves reviewing and possibly testing compliance with a funding agreement and may include:

- reviewing tasks performed by the recipient in conducting its activity, initiative or project
- testing the validity of any reports submitted
- assessing the internal controls related to the funding agreement
- reviewing eligibility of expenditures incurred by the recipient
- confirming that performance objectives defined in the funding agreement are being achieved.

The Treasury Board of Canada had been stressing the advantages of single recipient audit since the 1980s, namely that they could help eliminate duplication of audit efforts as well as clarify audit procedures of federal transfers to provincial governments. It was not until 2008, however, that the Auditor General of Canada called on the Government to implement a single audit process for recipients of transfer payments from federal programmes with the "2008 Directive on Transfer Payments". In 2010, the concept was further clarified with the "Guidelines on Recipient Audits Under the Policy on Transfer Payments and the Directive on Transfer Payments". The Guidelines define a single recipient audit as "**a co-ordinated approach to recipient auditing whereby an auditor representing some or all donors conducts a single recipient audit of a common recipient to verify compliance with terms and conditions of some or all funding agreements with that particular recipient.**"

Box 2.8. Reducing duplication and audit burden across levels of government *(continued)*

In order to co-ordinate single recipient audits, the Guidelines indicate that departmental managers should assess how many and how much of the funding agreements with any one recipient should be audited based on an assessment of risk. Furthermore, the Guidelines suggest an assessment of the costs/benefits of co-ordinating a single recipient audit, both within and among departments, taking into account for instance: the impact on the recipients operations, privacy concerns regarding sharing reports, and elements in funding agreements for shared audits.

Following this assessment, a department may try to promote the benefits of a single recipient audit with a recipient and ask the recipient to indicate other programmes or other associated departments with which it is dealing. With the recipient's agreement, the department then contacts other departments or programmes and suggests the possibility of a single recipient audit. The departmental Centre of Expertise for transfer payments, should it exist, may assist in the facilitation and co-ordination of single recipient audits.

United States' use of single audits for state and local governments

In the United States, the Single Audit Act of 1984 established requirements for audits of states, local governments, and Indian tribal governments that administer federal financial assistance programmes. In 1985, the Office of Management and Budget (OMB) issued OMB Circular A-128, "Audits of State and Local Governments," to provide implementing guidance. In 1990, OMB administratively extended the single audit process to non-profit organisations by issuing OMB Circular A-133, "Audits of Institutions of Higher Education and Other Non-Profit Organisations." In 1996 the Single Audit Act was amended to extend the statutory audit requirement to non-profit organisations.

Single audit in the United States is a combination of financial statement audits and compliance audits. All non-federal entities that expend USD 500 000 or more of federal awards in a year (USD 300 000 for fiscal year ending on or before 30 December 2003) are required to obtain an annual audit in accordance with the Single Audit Act Amendments of 1996, OMB Circular A-133, the OMB Circular Compliance Supplement and Government Auditing Standards. A single audit is intended to provide a cost-effective audit for non-federal entities in that one audit is conducted in lieu of multiple audits of individual programmes. This eliminates audit duplication and overlap by replacing multiple grant audits with a single financial and compliance audit of an entity covering all the recipient's funds and focusing on accounting and administrative internal controls. The Single Audits must be submitted to the Federal Audit Clearinghouse.

Before the single audit, administrative and audit costs were significantly higher because many entities receive awards from different federal agencies and were thus subject to a number of audits. The single audit then simplified this overlap by covering all the recipients' funds as well as focusing on accounting and administrative internal controls. The establishment of single audit also aimed to:

- improve the financial management of state and local governments receiving federal funds
- establish uniform requests for audits of federal financial assistance provided to state and local governments
- promote the efficient and effective use of audit resources
- ensure the federal departments and agencies, to the extent practicable, rely upon and use audit work done pursuant to the Act.

Evaluations of single audit submissions by the GAO reveal greater efficiencies, however with a continued need to ensure the quality of submissions is high.

Box 2.8. Reducing duplication and audit burden across levels of government *(continued)*

New Zealand's general purpose financial reports

Most public entities are formally required to produce general purpose financial reports that can be adapted to provide information both on financial performance and position and compliance.

The requirement to do this can be set by legislation, founding documents (such as trust deeds), the parent entity, or the responsible minister. General purpose financial reports are designed to provide financial and, where required, performance information to a range of users. To be relevant, the information must meet the accountability and/or decision-making needs of the users. The reports must follow predetermined guidelines for accounting standards and structure.

General purpose financial reports include financial and performance information

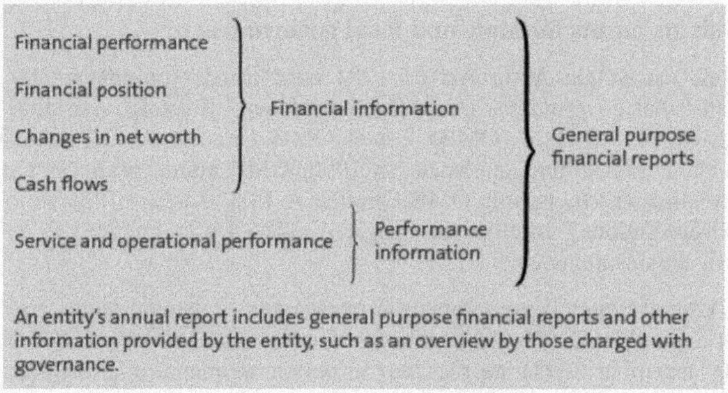

Source: Government of New Zealand (2016), "Part 1: Financial reporting in the public sector and why it matters", Controller and Auditor-General New Zealand, 24 February, www.oag.govt.nz/2016/financial-reporting/part1.htm?searchterm=purpose+reports.

Source: Government of Canada (2015), "Policy on Transfer Payments", www.tbs-sct.gc.ca/pol/doc-eng.aspx?id=13525; Directive on Transfer Payments: www.tbs-sct.gc.ca/pol/doc-eng.aspx?id=14208; Government of Canada (2010), "Guideline on Recipient Audits Under the Policy on Transfer Payments and the Directive on Transfer Payments", www.tbs-sct.gc.ca/pol/doc-eng.aspx?id=19061#fn18; OMB (n.d.), "Office of Federal Financial Management Single Audit", webpage, www.whitehouse.gov/omb/financial_fin_single_audit (accessed 18 September 2016); Government Accounting Office (1996), "Single Audit Refinements Can Improve Usefulness", GAO/T-AIMD-96-77, March; OMB (2015), "Circular A-133 Compliance Supplement 2015", www.whitehouse.gov/omb/circulars/a133_compliance_supplement_2015; Government of New Zealand (2016), "Part 1: Financial reporting in the public sector and why it matters", Controller and Auditor-General New Zealand, 24 February, www.oag.govt.nz/2016/financial-reporting/part1.htm?searchterm=purpose+reports.

A moderate pace of reform (i.e. medium to long term) is recommended as there are concerns about the ability of sub-national governments and institutions to be embrace the single-audit methodology and approach. Indeed, as discussed earlier, there is a wide dispersion of audit capacity in the states and municipalities, and at present not all would be prepared to apply the necessary accounting and auditing standards associated with such audits. This, coupled with the need to strengthen independence of audit institutions in some states, might suggest that the implementation of a single audit approach be first piloted, and that certain eligibility conditions be imposed. The latter could be tied into existing SNF initiatives, i.e. prior guarantee or certification of adequate legal harmonisation, satisfactory implementation of internal control policies, high levels of professionalisation, and so forth. An SNF working group on the matter could provide certifications and attestations of single audit eligibility.

Addressing key barriers to implementation of SNF initiatives for greater accountability

The SNF could improve its governance structure to enhance its effectiveness, better align strategic objectives and address areas of need, particularly in municipalities.

Mechanisms within the SNF itself could be strengthened to garner greater compliance from members and support more effective implementation of initiatives, particularly at the sub-national level. The SNF acts as a tool for vertical (between levels of government) and horizontal (between internal and external auditors) co-ordination. Several pre-existing co-ordination instruments were agglomerated under the SNF, including the National Association of State Audit Institutions for external audit entities (Asociación Nacional de Organismos de Fiscalización Superior y Control Gubernamental, or ASOFIS) and the Permanent Commission of Federal and State Comptrollers for internal control entities (Comisión Permanente de Contralores Estados – Federación, or CPCE-F). Both the CPCE-F and ASOFIS comprise smaller networks according to geographic regions.

In addition, the SNF maintains a Governance Board (Comité Rector) and various working groups, which facilitate both horizontal and vertical co-ordination across governments and entities. As summarised in Figure 2.4, the working groups include representatives from the Executive Branch (SFP), ASF, as well as state representatives. These groups work on specific initiatives and joint projects. Several OECD member and partner countries have similar co-ordination mechanisms in place, including Brazil, Canada and the United States that may be instructive (see Annex 2.A1 for detailed country examples).

Figure 2.4. **Working groups of the National Auditing System (SNF), as of September 2016**

Governing Committee (Comité Rector)

- Supreme organ of the SNF that serves a link with the SNA, and co-ordinates the other SNF's Working Groups; supports the implementation of the SNF's Auditing Professional Rules (Normas Profesionales de Auditoría del Sistema Nacional de Fiscalización).

Working Group on Professional Auditing Standards (Grupo de Trabajo sobre Normas Profesionales)

- Support the implementation of the SNF's Auditing Professional Rules (Normas Profesionales de Auditoría del Sistema Nacional de Fiscalización).

Working Group on Legal and Consulting Issues (Grupo de Trabajo Jurídico Consultivo)

- Formulating and receiving proposals in relation to the SNA.

Working Group on Internal Controls (Grupo de Trabajo sobre Control Interno)

- Harmonising the internal control legal framework throughout levels of government; ensuring the assessment of internal controls of auditing entities; identifying the legal changes needed to strengthen the internal control bodies of the Executive power.

Working Group on Governmental Accounting (Grupo de Trabajo sobre Contabilidad Gubernamental)

- Supporting the implementation of the General Law on Accounting (Ley General de Contabilidad Gubernamental) and other measures adopted by the National Council for Accounting Harmonisation (Consejo Nacional de Armonización Contable); establish the conditions to link the auditing and the audited entities; support municipalities in public accounting matters.

Working Group on Social Participation in the Oversight of Public Spending (Grupo de Trabajo sobre Participación Social en la Vigilancia del Gasto Público)

- Designing a strategy for auditing entities to follow up their oversight on entities benefitting from social funds and programmes; elaborating recommendations to strengthen the effective functioning of the social participation actors.

Participants in each working group:

- ASF and SFP, including the Auditor General and the Minister of Public Administration chair the Committee, and seven rotating members
- ASF and SFP (one representative each) and five rotating members from CPCE-F and ASOFIS

Source: Adapted from ASF (2015), "The Basis for Operations" [Bases Operativas para el Funcionamiento del SNF], published on 22 July 2015, www.snf.org.mx/bases-operativas-para-el-funcionamiento-del-snf-1.aspx.

Some improvements could be made in the governance structure and activities of the SNF to help make it a more effective co-ordination mechanism and address implementation gaps. Specifically, this could include improving strategic alignment between key actors (as discussed in Chapter 1), as well as improving the following:

- **Dedicated resources**: The Governing Board could consider a permanent Technical Secretariat to monitor progress on the strategic plan and support the work of the individual working groups and subnetworks of the SNF (i.e. CPCE-F and ASOFIS). Brazil's ATRICON, for example, (see Annex 2.A1) counts on such resources to support leadership.
- **Increased involvement of municipalities and other branches of government where the greatest weaknesses lie**: The SNF leadership could consider expanding the membership of the Governing Board to include, at least with observer status, representatives from municipalities and other branches of government that are currently under-represented (i.e. comptrollers from legislative and judicial branches, as well as state-owned enterprises). This would help increase buy-in from a key constituency, and help address a high-priority area largely unaddressed by the SNF. Similarly, SNF leadership may wish to consider expanding the size and representativeness of membership in working groups. Increasing the size of the various SNF groups, particularly by increasing the number of sub-national governments, could be beneficial in terms of getting greater buy-in on policies and facilitating implementation of approved initiatives. It would also be essential to reflect a greater diversity of views in the groups in order to identify any early legal and capacity gaps that should be considered in the design of policies and implementation plans.
- **Broader outreach to relevant constituencies**: The SNF could reach out to additional constituencies and create formal relationships with them, either as members of the SNF, observers or joint working groups. Canada's Council of Legislative Auditors for instance meets with public accounts committees, a key constituency for audit institutions, given the importance of congressional uptake of audit work in the accountability chain. Additional stakeholder might include professional associations of auditors and senate committees.
- **Leveraging additional co-ordination tools for multi-level governance**: Other mechanisms exist in Mexico to facilitate co-ordination between actors with shared goals and objectives. For instance, CONAGO (National Conference of Governors) and CONAMM (National Conference of Municipalities) play an important role in supporting the implementation of anti-corruption reforms at the state and local levels, and their engagement with SNF could help with implementation of reforms and developing buy-in among political leadership, as their membership includes senior leadership of sub-national institutions.
- **Increased monitoring of, and reporting on, results**: The binding nature of the agreements between members (e.g. *bases*, *convenios* and *acuerdos*) could be reinforced with the inclusion of specific output and outcome objectives, and more transparent monitoring and reporting to the Governing Committee and Congress. Monitoring could include comparative scorecards and indicators, for instance.
- **Increased frequency of meetings***:* The sharing of results occurs once per year in plenary meetings. The working groups employ virtual tools for conducting joint work, but more frequent meetings (e.g. at least biannual) could incentivise quicker progress.

State legislatures and the SNF could increase budgetary resources and address capacity gaps to help state audit institutions fulfil their mandates and mitigate the risk of disparities s across regions and levels of government.

SNF members face capacity and resource gaps that can further undermine implementation and ultimately the effectiveness of its initiatives. Such gaps arise naturally with the decentralisation and delegation of competences. Mexico faced the conundrum shared by many other OECD member and partner countries: is capacity at the sub-national level required before devolving competences from higher to lower levels of government, or is governance a "learning-by-doing" exercise where sub-national governments acquire capacity once they are faced with the responsibility of delivering on specific competences? (Charbit and Michalun, 2009). The latter approach of learning-by-doing has been the case in many states in Mexico. Nonetheless, capacity is not inherent, and it requires an investment of time and resources to develop.

State audit institutions (EFSEs) that do not prioritise training and professionalisation can fall into a vicious cycle, marked by "brain drain", poor performance, and as a result, ongoing difficulties in raising resources or attracting talent. Moreover, differences across states in terms of both capacities and resources can lead to varying outputs and quality between states, as well as growing divergences over time. Capacity is partly a function of the time employees stay at an organisation, assuming that institutions with less turnover have more institutional and technical knowledge, better problem-solving, greater efficiency and timeliness, and so forth. To help illustrate the capacity issues in EFSEs, Figure 2.5 shows the average number years of employment at each audit institution in 2012.

As shown in Figure 2.5, average years of employment vary widely by state, from less than 2 years in Aguascalientes to over 15 years in Baja California Sur. However, across states, the average year of employment is just over seven years. The turnover ratio is another indicator commonly used to assess capacity, providing information on the ability of an institution to retain institutional experience and knowledge over time. While some turnover is normal, and even positive for the organisation (i.e. a sign of adapting human resources to the evolving needs of the organisation), it can also suggest difficulties in retaining qualified staff and maintaining institutional memory and knowledge. High turnover can also threaten independence and objectivity if it is indicative of low job security. Turnover levels vary widely (from 0 to over 30 in Sinaloa).

Figure 2.5. **The average number of years of employment and turnover index in state audit institutions suggests capacity gaps in some Mexican states**

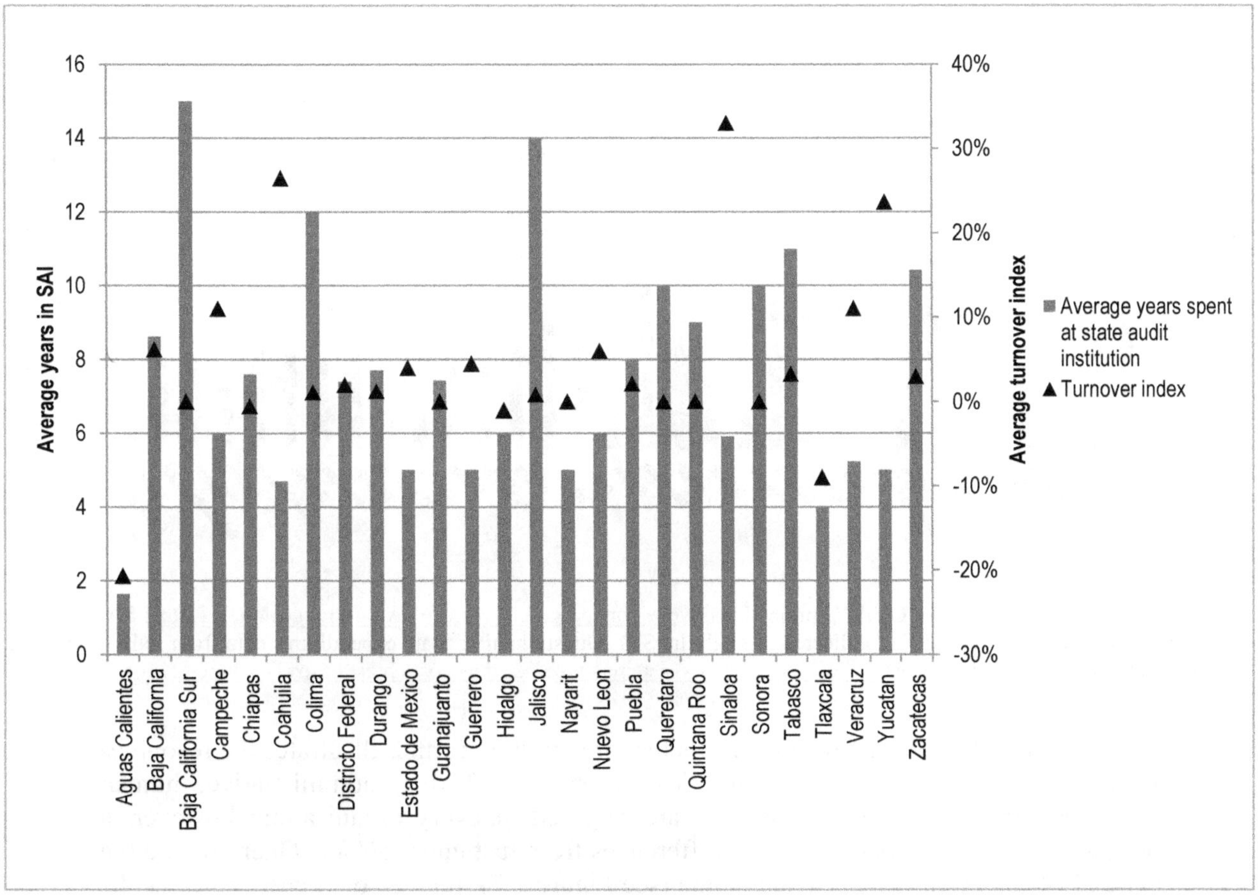

Note: This figure does not include data for Chihuaua, Michoacán, Morelos, Oaxaca or Tamaulipas.

Turnover index was calculated by subtracting employees who leave the organisation from the number of those joining the organisation within the same period. This figure is divided by the average number of total employees and multiplied by 100.

Source: Adapted from ASOFIS (2016), *Antecedentes*, database, www.asofis-basededatos.org.mx/.

Capacity challenges can arise when a capacity and fiscal gap intersect, especially when there is incoherence between the assignment of tasks and the provision of appropriate funding levels to accomplish these. If EFSEs are mandated with certain responsibilities, then they require the means to assume these, either from a budget increase, resources coming from higher levels of government, an ability to generate resources on its own or a combination of these. Figure 2.6 illustrates the budgets of EFSEs in relation to the state's population and expenditures, as a way to compare resources sub-nationally. Generally, across all states, EFSEs are under-resourced, and their budgets are low relative to the large scope of state expenditures they are expected to audit. Furthermore, a great deal of variation exists between EFSEs in terms of their resources, ranging from .01%-0.5% of state expenditures (see Figure 2.6).

Figure 2.6. **State audit institutions' budget per state capita and as a share of state expenditures highlights resource constraints**

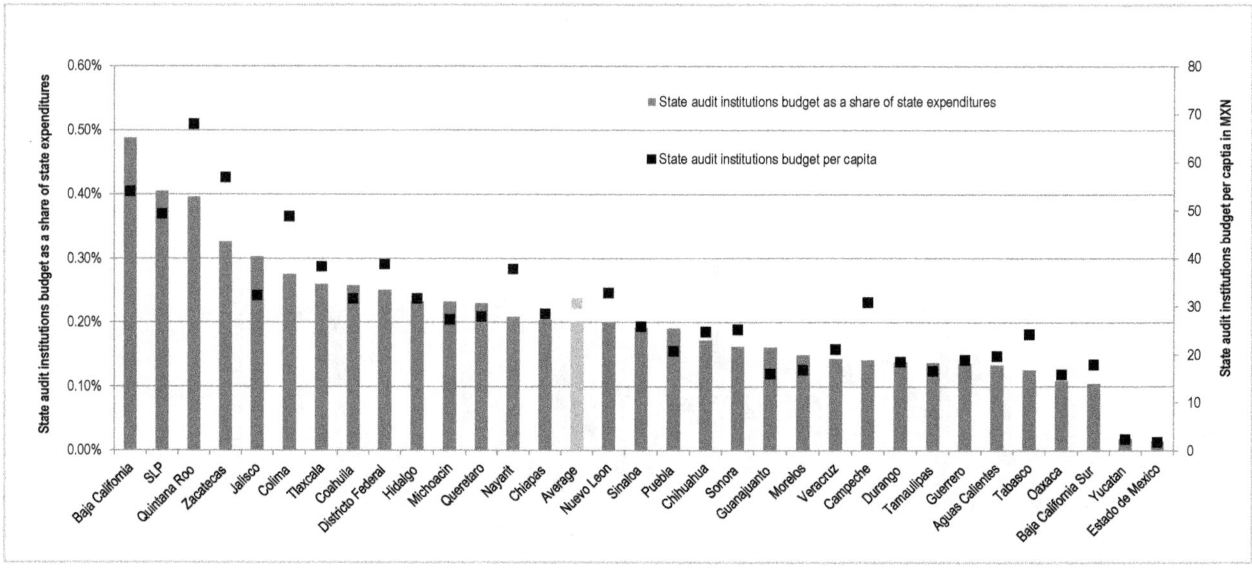

Source: Population data based on CONAPO projections, www.conapo.gob.mx/es/CONAPO/Proyecciones_Datos; SAI's budget data provided to the OECD by ASF as collected through the SNF Questionnaire; State expenditures data from INEGI database on state and municipal public finances, www3.inegi.org.mx/sistemas/tabuladosbasicos/tabtema.aspx?s=est&c=27565.

The share of total staff within EFSEs that are auditors further illustrates the resources available to tackle audit responsibilities. Support staff (e.g. administrative, human resources and information technology) are required in every organisation; however, a comparison across states reveals vast differences from just under 50% in Guerrero and the State of Mexico to nearly 90% in Colima (see Figure 2.7). It also potentially indicates the extent to which certain institutions outsource core audit work externally.

Figure 2.7. **Share of total staff in state audit institutions that are auditors suggest potential resource gaps in some Mexican states**

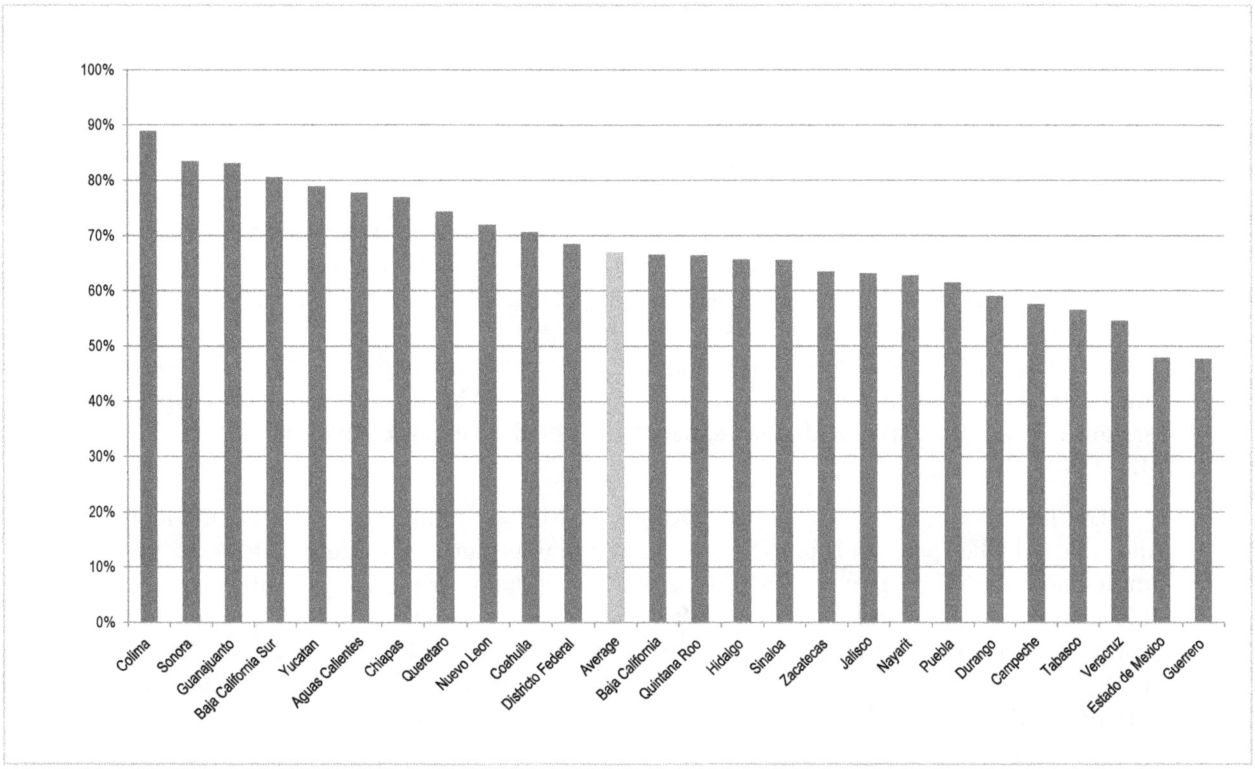

Source: Adapted from ASOFIS (2016), *Antecedentes*, database, www.asofis-basededatos.org.mx/.

Closing resource and capacity gaps are an urgent priority for the SNF, and they require scaling-up of current efforts. Specifically, the SNF could require:

- increasing budgetary resources for EFSEs, including grants to them for delegated audits, and with a vision to equalise funding and resources across states
- hiring of additional auditors with more competitive salaries
- professionalising the audit function, ensuring permanent positions and guaranteeing job security and independence of work (see next section)
- scaling-up training initiatives under the auspices of the SNF Working Group on Professionalisation to increase in-house capacities
- developing initiatives to increase mobility of auditors between EFSEs with a view to promote sharing of knowledge and good practices.

The SNF could strengthen the professional audit service and create sound human resource management policies in audit institutions that help to ensure independence and effective implementation of SNF initiatives.

The SNF may serve to further move sub-national governments to action and strengthen co-ordination mechanisms to promote and support activities, but the main implementation burden remains nonetheless in the hands of sub-national institutions. The implementation of SNF initiatives and priorities therefore can be derailed by major capacity gaps within the system. These gaps, particularly present at sub-national levels, include a lack of human capital, knowledge and financial resources. Even the best-intentioned institutions and managers can fall short of meeting reform expectations if the necessary resources are unavailable.

The effectiveness of audit institutions rests in large part on the quality of their human capital. Audits require high levels of technical competence (e.g. accounting, financial management and audit methodologies) as well as knowledge in specific policy sectors (e.g. education, environment, health, and the economy). Therefore, public auditors must specialise, but also continually develop and improve their skills, knowledge, and working methods. The capacity-building process is a key element to improve the work of SAIs, and represents a priority for INTOSAI, which deals with such issues through a specific committee (Capacity Building Committee). As discussed in Chapter 1, INTOSAI's guide identifies three aspects of capacity building for an SAI: professional audit capacity, organisational capacity, and the capacity to deal with the external environment (INTOSAI, 2007b).

The professionalisation of public auditing in Mexico remains an ongoing challenge, and one of the principal barriers to strengthening audit functions and effectively implementing SNF initiatives. Several factors contribute to this. Firstly, as noted earlier in this chapter, national reforms to standardise the mandate and work of external audit institutions in states occurred fairly recently, and therefore professionalisation of auditors in these institutions remains an ongoing process. Similarly, analogous legislation for internal auditors in sub-national levels of government can also be relatively new; however, this can vary by state, since state congresses are responsible for such legislation.

Second, high levels of turnover of public auditors, particularly at sub-national levels but also at the federal level, further hinder professionalisation efforts. Until 2014, when Mexico passed a constitutional reform, mayors (*presidentes municipales*) were not permitted to be re-elected immediately following their three-year term. This ordinarily would not be a barrier for strengthening capacities were it not for the common practice in Mexico of new mayors removing incumbent officials from their posts, including auditors, and hiring new staff. This practice, which varies in frequency across states and municipalities, is partly due to a culture of political loyalty and affiliation in the country. This ultimately makes it difficult to establish a core cadre of professional auditors that are recruited and promoted based on merit, with job security and opportunities for continual development and learning. For internal auditors in the executive branch, the extension of the civil service regime (Servicio Profesional de Carrera) is still in progress. Furthermore, even for external auditors, there is a similar tendency at the state level, since the Constitution (Article 116) dictates that governors may not be re-elected following their six-year terms. Again, while this varies by state, the tendency has been for newly elected leadership to replace public auditors in their positions, particularly when there is a change in the political party in power.

As a result the generation of institutional knowledge is cyclical and resources invested in training/capacity building can be sunk costs following an election. The SNF has in place a Working Group on Professional Auditing Standards (see Box 2.9), which has developed standards aligned with those of INTOSAI, the IIA and International Federation of Accountants (IFAC) and is tasked with harmonising standards across the system. These are promoted through capacity-building efforts, such as trainings and certifications.

Box 2.9. SNF Working Group on Professional Auditing Standards

The SNF Working Group on Professional Auditing Standards has been tasked with determining the professional standards for public auditors across levels of government. The standards, which were published in 2014, are extensive and cover such topics as: institutional objectives and responsibilities; criteria for ensuring independence; ethics and code of conduct; audit typologies, methodologies and quality assurance; capacity building; inter-institutional co-ordination and information sharing; guidelines for outsourcing; and transparency and communications.

More specific standards are set out for financial, performance and compliance audits, detailing scope and concrete elements that should be included; evidence, documentation, risk management, formats for publishing results; and follow-up on audit findings and recommendations.

Source: SNF (2014), "Normas Profesionales de Auditoría de Sistema Nacional de Fiscalización", SNF Publishing, www.snf.org.mx/normas-profesionales-1.aspx.

Furthermore, the federal government is planning to support the capacity-building process of state audit institutions by allocating specific resources to improve and harmonise government accounting. In particular, Article 41 of the Draft Budget Law for the Fiscal Year 2016 allocates specific resources to the training and professionalisation of the administrative units responsible for government accounting, as well as to modernise information and communication technologies. This effort will assist in accomplishing accounting harmonisation throughout the three branches of government, in line with the General Law on Government Accounting.

However, the SNF faces an uphill battle in the sense that the results of these efforts can be undermined every few years with the turnover of the governor or mayor. Therefore, while capacity-building efforts are worthwhile and should be maintained and scaled up, the SNF Working Group on Professional Auditing Standards should also strongly consider supporting the implementation of good human resource management (HRM) policies that build a more permanent and competent workforce of public auditors. This would entail new work (e.g. guidelines, tools and targeted trainings) on the HRM practices of internal and external audit institutions, focusing on merit-based recruiting and promotion, evaluation of performance and capacity building.

SNF members could address the "implementation gap" related to internal control and risk management activities by conducting audits and evaluations that encourage ownership, accountability and skill development among public sector managers responsible for these functions.

Internal control and risk management practices are integral functions for fostering accountability. Managers at all levels of organisations are responsible for, and may be required to explain, the decisions and actions taken to meet the objectives of the organisation they manage. Managerial control and accountability implies responsibility for sound performance and financial management. For managers of executive branch entities, this includes responsibilities for the design and execution of internal control systems and risk-management functions, as well reporting of the results of such efforts. The latter can be seen as a democratic principle, relating directly to strengthening the transparency of government actions and policies.

The fact that ASF and SFP use different frameworks for internal control and risk management can be problematic on its own, as discussed above; however, an implementation gap exists in Mexican public sector entities regardless of which framework used. The gap refers to the need for greater integration of internal control and risk-management practices into the everyday management of government entities in Mexico, in accordance with international standards and guidelines like the International Organisation for Standardisation (ISO) 3100, COSO's Enterprise Risk Management-Integrated Framework and the UK HM Treasury's Orange Book on Management of Risks. Internal control and risk management in Mexico's government entities is considered "ad hoc," as opposed to integrated into organisational objectives and day-to-day operations. In general, integration of internal control and risk management into strategic and operational planning processes is mostly done on a nominal basis as part of a methodological exercise.

Both SFP and ASF have conducted reviews and developed tools in an effort to improve the implementation of internal control and risk-management processes and procedures in executive branch agencies. The SFP, as the internal audit function and "third line of defence," is responsible for assessing the efficiency and the effectiveness of current arrangements, providing assurance about the maturity of the internal control system, the extent of integration and quality of implementation. SFP proposes actions to improve the capacity of public administration to conduct these activities. Moreover, the SFP's Administrative Guide for the Implementation of the Internal Control System provides (see Article 3, Title 2, Chapter IV) for an annual self-evaluation exercise of the internal control arrangements inside the federal entities in order to assess the degree of implementation of different components, as well as identify weaknesses and opportunities for corrective actions.

The Internal Control Organs of SFP (Órganos Internos de Control, or OIC) are responsible for reviewing answers to the self-evaluations and the supporting documentation. In a sense, the OICs perform the role of an internal audit function, providing assurance to the management of the quality of the internal control processes. The whole process is supported by a toolkit of analytical criteria (Criterios para la Evaluación del Órgano Interno de Control al Informe Anual del Estado que Guarda el Sistema de Control Interno Institucional). These reports can also provide external auditors additional assurance on the effectiveness of the internal audit department as an entity-level control.

In addition to the efforts of the SFP and OICs to improve implementation of internal control and risk-management functions, ASF published its own comprehensive self-assessment models based on COSO's Internal Control-Integrated Framework and the lessons learned from its studies, including those mentioned above (Studies No. 1172 and No. 1198). They include a Model of Evaluation of Internal Control in Municipal Public Administration (Study No. 1212, February 2015) and a Model of Evaluation of Internal Control in Central Public Administration, issued in April 2015. The self-evaluations of both ASF and SFP are meant to apply across, and at, different levels of government.

One main challenge is ensuring that managers in the executive branch fully understand the need, and have a strong commitment to integrating the internal control functions across the organisation. To this end, the SNF could further explore the benefits, opportunities and constraints to link the implementation and integration of the internal control system, including the risk-management function, with the budget execution and the disbursement of fiscal resources. This could allow managers to use the maturity of the internal control components as a performance and assurance indicator that the entity is working to enhance integrity, manage risks and safeguard fiscal resources to strengthen accountability and governance.

External audits and self-evaluations suggest progress on implementing existing internal control standards, yet full alignment is inconsistent across government. As an example, the Figure 2.8 depicts the results of ASF's 2012 and 2013 assessments of the degree of implementation of the different internal control components by federal public entities.

Figure 2.8. **Implementation of internal control components in Mexico shows progress but potential for improvement**

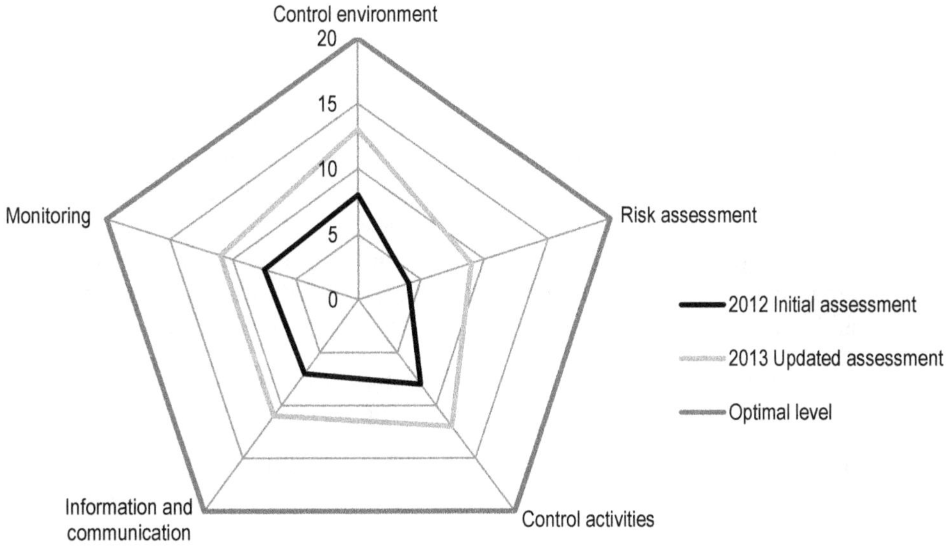

Source: Adapted from ASF's Study No. 1198, "Continuidad a los Estudios de Control Interno y a la Difusión del Estudio de Integridad en el Sector Público." The updated assessments are based on the additional evidence provided by the institutions (2013).

The outer line (light blue) represents an optimal level of each component of internal control and risk management. The difference between this line and the others reflects the degree of suboptimal performance when implementing the different components. The Comptroller General of the Republic of Peru (CGR) followed a similar methodological approach. In 2013 and 2014, the CGR undertook two major reviews of the degree of implementation of the Internal Control System across state entities. The reviews also involved self-assessment exercises, including questionnaires, based on the methodological and practical guidelines provided by the CGR. The main findings are reflective of challenges Mexico faces and may be instructive:

- There was a significant gap between the maturity levels of central government compared to regional and local institutions. There are also disparities between different regions.

- The weakest component was risk management. Many entities did not seem to understand the significance of this process and they did not identify their risks. When they do, they are often failing to implement activities to mitigate those risks.
- Similarly, officials struggled to understand the importance of internal control as an integrated part of daily management and a valuable tool to attain their objectives, fight corruption, restore trust and provide better services to the citizens.
- Agencies, autonomous bodies and municipal enterprises scored better than other organisations.
- State-owned enterprises (SOEs) scored very well during the evaluation exercise. These entities have to apply corporate governance codes, which states that there should be audit committees. Furthermore, the codes require SOEs to put in place risk-management systems.

Addressing the implementation gap will be critical for the SNF, particularly ASF and SFP, in order for there to be effective internal control and risk management in Mexico's public sector. Regardless of the standards used, failing to address this gap threatens the government's ability to achieve the key goals of recent constitutional reforms. Moreover, this issue has implications for multiple levels of government, since states and municipalities face the same challenges of implementing effective internal control and risk-management systems. To help close the implementation gap, entities within the SNF can consider audits and evaluations that help strengthen the following:

- integrating individual tasks in relation to internal control and risk management with the institution's objectives and strategic plans
- linking reward systems (e.g. remuneration, promotion) with the performance of specific and measurable duties within the internal control function
- incorporating in the individual job descriptions for specific high-risk processes (e.g. procurement, payroll) and concrete obligations in relation to the management and the ownership of controls and risks
- training and awareness campaigns focusing on clarifying the tasks and the responsibilities within the internal control system between the personnel working at the operational level ("first line of defence") and those who have no direct operational responsibility, thus being independent from delivery units ("second line of defence")
- communicating and reporting (e.g. newsletters, website, and posters) specific cases of detected control weaknesses, and actions taken to remedy the situation, including any sanctions applied as well as appraisals and awards related to specific initiatives and actions to improve the control and risk functions.

Box 2.10 provides additional information from the European perspective for ASF and SFP to consider for improving management control over government resources to strengthen integrity.

Box 2.10. **Guidance for monitoring the effectiveness of internal control and risk-management systems**

The Federation of European Risk Management Associations (FERMA) and European Confederation of Institutes of Internal Auditing (ECIIA) Guidance on the 8th European Company Law Directive on Statutory Audit offers key points for thinking about the implementation of a sound system of monitoring the effectiveness of internal control, internal audit and risk-management systems. It includes the following questions:

1. Who monitors the adequacy of the internal control system? Are there processes to review the adequacy of financial and other key controls for all new systems, projects and activities?

A key part of any effective internal control system is a mechanism to provide feedback on how the systems and processes are working so that shortfalls and areas for improvement can be identified and changes implemented. In the first instance if there is an internal control department, it will help managers implement sound internal controls. The operation of key controls will then be subject to review by internal and external audit along with other review agencies, both internal and external to the organisation. If no internal control department exists, guidance may be sought from risk management or internal audit.

2. Are arrangements in place to assess periodically the effectiveness of the organisation's control framework?

A key requirement of many of the internal control requirements encompassed in legislation throughout the European Union and the rest of the world is an annual attestation as to the adequacy and effectiveness of the internal control system. Such attestation should be clearly evidenced. The review of the control framework will be the responsibility of the audit committee who will receive information and assurances from internal audit, risk management and the external auditors.

3. Who assesses internal audit?

The audit committee assesses the performance of the internal audit function by receiving performance information from the function itself and consulting appropriate directors and the external auditors. In addition, the function should be independently reviewed by an external agency such as the Institute of Internal Auditors (IIA), as specified in the International Professional Practices Framework, issued by the IIA.

4. How are the proposed audit activities prioritised? Is the determination linked to the organisations' risk-management plan and internal audit's own risk assessment? Are the internal audit plan and budget challenged when presented?

The work of internal audit should be set out in a risk-based plan challenged and approved annually by the audit committee. This plan should be informed by the work of other review agencies such as external audit and risk management and should contain sufficient work for the head of internal audit to be able to form an overall view as to the adequacy of the risk-management process operated by the organisation. If there is no formal risk-management process or if the process is flawed, then internal audit will need to rely on some other method of assessing the key activities and controls for its review. This could be based on its own risk assessment.

Source: FERMA-ECIIA (2014), "Guidance on the 8th EU Company Law Directive", www.ferma.eu/about/publications/eciia-ferma-guidance/.

Proposals for action

Mexico's National Auditing System (Sistema Nacional de Fiscalización, or SNF) enjoys a pre-existing institutional architecture to strengthen co-ordination and collaboration; however, further efforts could be instituted to close "gaps" that can derail large-scale reforms and undermine the public's confidence in government. Chief among those are legal and policy gaps that threaten independence and coherence of auditing in Mexico. **Specifically, the SNF could close legal and policy gaps to improve the independence of sub-national external and internal audit institutions in Mexico. The SNF could also advance a coherent, government-wide approach to internal control and risk management by harmonising existing frameworks and improving co-ordination between external and internal audit bodies. In addition, over the medium to long term, the SNF could simplify audit procedures for sub-national levels of government to minimise duplication and help ASF to effectively manage its expanded mandate to audit revenue-sharing transfers.** Building momentum around each of these legal and policy gaps will take time. Addressing each of these legal and policy gaps would help to enhance the effectiveness of the SNF as a system, and provide concrete objectives to motivate collaboration among SNF members.

For the SNF to be effective, it should consider key barriers to implementation and take steps to address them. These barriers largely refer to capacity and implementation gaps at all levels of government. Some of these gaps occur within the SNF itself, and could provide a quick win to begin addressing some of the more challenging issues SNF members face. **For instance, the SNF could improve its governance structure to enhance its effectiveness, better align strategic objectives and address areas of need, particularly in municipalities.** In addition, other implementation gaps refer directly to the need for additional resources and capacity at the sub-national level. In particular, **state legislatures and the SNF could consider scaling up budgetary resources and addressing capacity gaps in states where there is the greatest need in order to help state audit institutions fulfil their mandates and mitigate the risk of disparities across regions and levels of government. The SNF could also strengthen the professional audit service and create sound human resource management policies in audit institutions that help to ensure independence and effective implementation of SNF initiatives.** Finally, some implementation gaps highlight the need for improvements to the carrying out of audit work in a coherent, unified manner. **In the Mexican context, this could entail SNF members addressing the "implementation gap" related to internal control and risk management activities by conducting audits and evaluations that encourage ownership, accountability and skill development among public sector managers responsible for these functions.**

Annex 2.A1

Illustrating multi-level co-ordination with selected cases

Australasian Council of Auditors-General (ACAG)

The Australasian Council of Auditors-General (ACAG) is an association established by Auditors-General for their mutual support and for sharing of information. Membership is open to the Auditors-General of all jurisdictions in Australia, New Zealand, Fiji and Papua New Guinea. Associate membership and observer status may be accorded to any eligible jurisdiction. Through membership in ACAG, members benefit from a convenient means of mutual support, ready access to peer groups and individuals within the ACAG community, access to industry intelligence, an awareness of emerging issues, ideas, problems and solutions, and tools to improve the efficiency and effectiveness of member offices.

As the core resource, ACAG relies on staff time and expertise of ACAG member offices to participate in the development of agreed submissions to standard-setters and parliamentary committees and to provide resources for the voluntary quality assurance reviews of audit offices. Similarly, ACAG member offices manage an annual benchmarking process, client and parliamentarian satisfaction surveys, and also maintain and deliver training.

The Executive Committee, which is comprised of three members, endorses the annual work plan and budget prior to it being confirmed by the ACAG members. It also performs a management role between meetings of members with the main purposes being to guide and monitor the activities of the part-time Executive Director, to monitor achievement of ACAG's objectives and to report to ACAG members on its deliberations. Members meet half yearly and the Executive Director of the Secretariat co-ordinates activities and meetings.

The Executive Director provides the secretariat function, which can leverage the support as needed from time to time by staff of the audit office that hosts ACAG. The work of the Secretariat includes developing and executing the annual work plan and organising the twice-yearly meeting of members and assisting with organising two other international meetings that occur every two years. In addition, the Secretariat provides support for ACAG sub-groups and working parties and facilitates the sharing of information locally and internationally. It also liaises with external stakeholders and co-ordinates ACAG submissions to public inquiries into matters of public sector accountability and related questions.

There are currently four ACAG sub-groups and working parties. The Heads of the Performance Audit Group arrange sharing of information; support development of performance audit methods and practices; identify possible concurrent (collaborative) audit topics and agree on the audit objectives, lines of inquiry and criteria; arrange performance audit training for staff; and arrange for the external review of performance audit reports on request. The Financial Reporting and Auditing Committee (FRAC) provides ACAG with strategic and technical advice on developments in accounting, financial reporting and auditing; and makes submissions to standard-setters on accounting, auditing and related matters. The Heads of the Financial Audit Group share information regarding the practice and management of the financial audit function. The ACAG Information Systems (IS) Audit Group is a forum for exchange of knowledge and experience in information technology (IT) audit and use of IT as a support tool for auditors. Finally, the Audit Quality Assurance Panel assists audit offices to meet requirements for quality control by providing an approach to internal quality reviews and organising external reviews on request; manages the arrangements by which audit offices can benchmark their operations; and manages the arrangements by which audit offices can participate in client and parliamentarian satisfaction surveys.

ACAG is also active in co-ordinating audits across its members. For ACAG, concurrent (collaborative) audits are a strategic response to the stakeholder expectations emerging from changes in the Australian federal/state relations toward a more co-operative federalism. They are a primary means of sharing and leveraging the expertise, knowledge and experience of all Australasian Audit Offices and a practical means of providing greater added value through "the whole being greater than the sum of the parts".

At present, legislation governing public sector audit in each of the Australasian jurisdictions typically places practical limits on audit collaboration except for performance audits. In selecting a concurrent performance audit topic, it was agreed that not every state/territory office needs to participate in every audit but every proposed audit should include the Australian National Audit Office. Also, possible topics need to be settled well in advance in order to get them onto an office's forward programme where these have to be negotiated with the relevant local parliamentary committee.

The lessons learnt from the one collaborative audit completed so far include:

- Each participating office needs to understand the constraints which their partners work under as each office has a different mandate and operates under different legislation.
- Client agencies will communicate with one another across jurisdictional boundaries so each participating office needs to be well prepared.
- Present constraints mean that most collaboration is largely limited to sharing of planning and research information and sharing of methodologies (sources of criteria, sampling, fieldwork sites, managing scope and consultation).
- For continuous improvement it is important to evaluate the collaborative approach at completion and document the lessons learnt.

Brazil's Association of Courts of Audit of Brazil (ATRICON)

Brazil is composed of 26 States, one Federal District and 5570 municipalities. Similarly to the NAS in Mexico therefore, in Brazil, federal, state and municipal external audit institutions coordinate through the Association of Courts of Audit of Brazil (ATRICON), which was created in 1992 in order to strengthen relationships between

Courts of Audit through the design and implementation of tools to enhance control systems and facilitate the exchange of information between institutions. ATRICON works in close partnership with the Institute Rui Barbosa (IRB, ATRICON internal think tank), and the Brazilian Association of Municipal Audit Courts (ABRACOM), as well as a series of national professional associations (the National Associations of Auditors, Public Prosecution Service Accounts, College of Prosecutors and Ombudsmen of the Audit Court of Brazil). ATRICON counts with a permanent Secretariat of about 10 staff to help support initiatives.

Elected every two years, the ATRICON Board sets, in consultation with members, the Association's strategic goals and actions. The 2012-2017 strategic plan includes measures for: citizen engagement and external communication, strengthening information-sharing between members, increasing audit transparency, quality control measures for audits, and supporting knowledge-sharing and capacity-building. Second, ATRICON works in sector-specific policy areas including: infrastructure and education.

Furthermore, the TCU itself- through ATRICON- utilises both joint and coordinated audits. Similar to the Convenios between ASF and individual States, the TCU enters into bilateral agreements with both States and Municipalities for a set of pre-determined scope of audits. Recent joint work has centred on social security regimes, quality of education facilities and health systems. Cooperation agreements between the TCU and the different states and municipalities involved are detailed listing the audit scope, methodology, resources, planning (including pilot audits), the databases/information to be used, etc. A recent 2013 coordinated audit on high school education for instance included 90 auditors from the TCU working jointly with State and municipal audit staff.

The Canadian Council of Legislative Auditors (CCOLA)

The Canadian Council of Legislative Auditors (CCOLA) is an organisation devoted to sharing information, building consensus, and supporting the continued development of auditing methodology, practices and professional development among legislative audit offices at the federal and provincial levels. Its membership consists of the federal Auditor General and Auditors General of each of the ten Canadian provinces.[5] Legislative auditors from outside of Canada can have either "Associate Member" status with full voting rights, or "Observer Member" status which does not afford voting rights.[6] The CCOLA currently has one associate member – the Auditor General of Bermuda, and one observer member – the Auditor General of the Cayman Islands.

The CCOLA is funded from member offices, based on a mutually agreed upon formula. Along with the funding formula, the CCOLA members annually review and agree upon the budget. CCOLA funding is used primarily to support the CCOLA Secretariat, its various committees and groups, and to sponsor conferences and symposiums.

The CCOLA also works with the Canadian Council of Public Accounts Committees (CCPAC) and the Canadian Council of Comptrollers. The CCPAC facilitates the exchange of information and experience relating to Public Accounts Committees across Canada, and works with provincial and federal Auditors General to improve the effectiveness of both the Auditors and the Public Accounts Committees. The Canadian Council of Comptrollers facilitates the sharing and exchange of information and experience among the federal, provincial and territorial comptrollers.

The CCOLA and its committees and groups meet throughout the year either in person or remotely to further their respective annual plans. In addition, each year the CCOLA sponsors three main events: the Financial Statement Symposium and Public Accounts Forum; the Performance Audit Symposium; and the CCPAC-CCOLA Annual Conference. Every four years the CCOLA also sponsors the ACAG-CCOLA Forum in Canada with the Australasian Council of Auditors-General.

Organisational structure and collaboration

Seven committees, which include the Planning and Co-ordinating Committee (PCC), the Strategic Matters Committee (SMC) and five CCOLA Strategic Support Committees, along with seven Information Sharing Groups support the work of the CCOLA. The PCC facilitates the activities of the CCOLA, manages the CCOLA's administrative and financial affairs, including the development of the business plan, and monitors the achievement of the CCOLA's objectives. The PCC is comprised of three Auditors General based on an agreed upon rotation schedule. Each member is appointed for a three-year term, typically, the first year as member, the second year as the Vice Chair and the third year as the Chair. The SMC provides the CCOLA with a means to track its risks and opportunities, and as directed by the CCOLA, oversees key CCOLA activities and/or priorities. The SMC also serves as an avenue by which the CCOLA encourages initiatives for collaboration via joint and concurrent audits, such as reviews, studies or follow-up work; and through capacity assistance, such as sharing staff between offices, and information, advice sharing and training on areas of interest.

Collaboration among the federal and provincial audit offices is also achieved through the CCOLA Strategic Support Committees and Information Sharing Groups. The Strategic Support Committees have mandates that are related to areas that are of critical importance to the core functioning of CCOLA and its member offices, such as audit training, human resources management (HRM), IT and peer reviews. The Information Sharing Groups research, discuss and share information and co-ordinate audits and activities with respect to specific sectoral issues of common interest to member offices, such as environment, education, governance, health, infrastructure and justice.

The CCOLA Secretariat is provided to CCOLA as an in-kind contribution by the Office of the Auditor General of Canada (OAG). The Secretariat's responsibilities are approved by CCOLA. The Secretariat provides administrative support to the CCOLA, the PCC, the strategic support committees and limited support to Information Sharing Groups, in the fulfilment of their responsibilities.

Two significant CCOLA collaborative efforts include the CCOLA's Training and Capacity Development Initiative (TCDI). The goal of the TCDI is to leverage the training resources available in each member office to develop and maintain CCOLA competency models, curriculums and course calendars for financial, performance and IT audits and soft skills. Additionally, the CCOLA is undertaking a Collaborative Climate Change Audit, an initiative agreed to in principle in August 2015 with the project charter approved in April 2016 by all CCOLA partners.

The Contact Committee and the European Court of Auditors

The European Union represents a unique environment for external public audit and audit-related co-operation at supra-national level. Member state supreme audit institutions

(SAIs) and the European Court of Auditors (ECA) co-operate within a specific platform – the Contact Committee. The Contact Committee, established in the 1960s, is an informal, non-binding and apolitical assembly of the Heads of Member State SAIs and the ECA. It provides a forum for co-operation and exchange of professional knowledge and experience on the audit of EU funds and other EU-related issues. It is not a part of the EU structures and does not establish a hierarchical relationship between its members. The equality of opinion of its members is underlined by the fact that decisions are made by consensus. The Contact Committee receives neither funding nor direction from third parties and has no permanent chair – the chairmanship rotates on an annual basis.

The Contact Committee meets once a year to discuss recent developments and matters of common interest and to agree on activities to be carried out. If necessary, it communicates its position on relevant issues to third parties. Day-to-day contacts are maintained through the liaison officers appointed by each institution. Working groups, networks and taskforces are used to carry out co-ordinated audits, as well as to develop common positions and practices for issues of common interest. They address issues such as the use of the EU's Structural Funds, value-added tax and the prevention and combating of irregularities and fraud. They also deal with fiscal policy issues, the Europe 2020 Strategy, national SAI reports on EU financial management, independent assessments of national public economic policies as well as the European Public Sector Accounting Standards (EPSAS).

Audit work is an important part of Contact Committee co-operation. The three collaborative audits currently under way concern the contribution of Structural Funds to the Europe 2020 strategy in the area of education and employment, the underlying risks for the sustainability of public finances, and the implementation of prudential supervision of banks.

The specific role of the ECA

The mission of the ECA is to contribute to improving EU financial management, promote accountability and transparency, and act as the independent guardian of the financial interests of the citizens of the European Union. As the European Union's independent external auditor, the ECA's role is to check that EU funds are correctly accounted for, are raised and spent in accordance with the relevant rules and regulations and have achieved value for money. The ECA operates as a collegiate body of 28 members, one from each member state. The members are appointed by the European Council after consultation of the European Parliament for a renewable term of six years. Members elect one of their number as president for a renewable term of three years.

The Treaty on the Functioning of the European Union requires the ECA and national audit bodies of the member states to co-operate in a spirit of trust, while maintaining their independence. Co-operation between the SAIs of the EU member states and the ECA dates back to the beginning of the Court's existence in 1977, and has increased over the years. Co-operation between EU member state SAIs and the ECA is not simply a legal obligation but rather a practical necessity dictated by the fact that the EU and national administrations have become more and more closely linked. With the large-scale decentralisation of the management of the EU budget towards the national authorities in the member states and beneficiary countries, the centre of gravity of the audit of EU money has moved towards these countries. In practice, the national supreme audit institutions provide the ECA's auditors with local practical and logistical support as well as specific knowledge of the audited field.

The ECA voluntarily provides the Contact Committee with administrative support, including notably the administration of the Contact Committee website, the collection and distribution of information, and administrative assistance to the Contact Committee, its chair and the liaison officers in performing their tasks. Furthermore, the ECA hosts and chairs a Contact Committee meeting every third year.

Co-operation with candidate and potential candidate countries

The Contact Committee promotes co-operation between its members and the SAIs of candidate and potential candidate countries. The co-operation is mainly channelled through the Network of the SAIs of EU Candidate and Potential Candidate Countries ("the Network"), of which the ECA is a member. Most Network activities are carried out in partnership with SIGMA (Support for Improvement in Governance and Management), a joint initiative of the OECD and the European Union, and the Contact Committee Joint Working Group on Audit Activities, which provides professional, organisational and technical advice and support.

The Network operates similarly to the Contact Committee. It involves periodic meetings of the heads of SAIs and liaison officers, as well as working groups, seminars, workshops and parallel audits. It is also independent and receives neither funding nor direction from the Contact Committee or third parties. The ECA's specific assistance includes direct support to the Network activities, an internship programme for the auditors from the SAIs concerned, and the possibility for their auditors to attend a selection of ECA's internal training courses.

The US National Intergovernmental Audit Forum

In existence for over 40 years, the National Intergovernmental Audit Forum (the National Forum) in the United States is an association of audit executives from federal, state, and local governments (National Intergovernmental Audit Forum, 2016). It exists to improve co-ordination, communication, and co-operation among its members, private sector firms, and other accountability organisations to address common challenges; enhance government performance, accountability, and transparency; and increase public trust. Annual meetings provide the opportunity to exchange information on current and emerging issues, best practices, auditing standards and facilitate networking among members of the audit community. Such meetings also provide professional education to those with audit responsibilities at each level of government (federal, state and local) in the United States. Those attending a typical meeting lead or staff: 1 of 72 Federal Inspectors General recognised by the Inspector General Act of 1978 as amended;[7] an audit office from one of 56 state and territories;[8] or an audit organisation at the local level, where there are over 90 000 government entities.[9]

Historically, the implications of key developments in intergovernmental relations for auditors led to the creation of the National Forum and ten regional audit forums in 1973 and 1974. The US General Accounting Office (now the US Government Accountability Office [GAO]) with the assistance of key organisations representing different levels of government[10] wanted to provide the audit community with the ability to address the requirements of new legislation and new auditing standards. Statutes such as the Intergovernmental Cooperation Act of 1968 sought to improve the administration of federal grants and share federal revenues with state and local governments. New auditing standards also had important implications for federal, state and local governments. In

1972, GAO published a set of auditing standards for government agencies (known as the "Yellow Book").[11]

The charter for the National Forum establishes its leadership and membership structure as well as operating procedures. Its Executive Committee consists of public sector audit executives and associate members interested in furthering the National Forum's mission and goals. It is comprised of two Federal Inspectors General; two State members; two local members; two associate members, with one representing certified public accounting firms; and a representative from the US Office of Management and Budget. The Committee is chaired by the Comptroller General of the United States and head of GAO. In addition to the Comptroller General, members of the forum consist of the following audit executives: all federal Inspectors General subject to the Inspector General Act, as amended; heads of state audit organisations, up to three from each regional forum selected by the state auditors of that region; and heads of local audit organisations, up to three from each regional forum selected by the local auditors of that region. Besides playing a leadership role, GAO makes significant contributions of human capital and other resources critical to leading the National Forum. This includes serving as the primary organiser of the National Forum's annual meeting held either in Washington, DC or in other locations. The organisation is financed by meeting participant registrations with over 930 registrations since 2010.

In recent meetings, the National Forum and regional audit forums have fostered dialogue and collaboration on current and emerging issues of common interest within the accountability community. Recent meetings have featured speakers and panels including risk-related trends such as cybersecurity; data analytics for identifying improper payments in areas such as Medicaid-managed care; developments such as "smart cities" and the Internet of Things; e-government and digital best practices and the implications of key statutes such as the Digital Accountability and Transparency Act. Recent National Forum meetings have also advanced audit standards and shared best practices enhancing the capacity, effectiveness, and professionalism of audit organisations. In addition, the National Forum has featured GAO's new Fraud Risk Management Framework[12] as well as government-wide initiatives on enterprise risk management. Speakers are drawn from senior officials in the intergovernmental accountability community as well as thought leaders in public administration, representatives of industry, users of audit reports, and other organisations. In recent years, meetings have featured the Governor of Colorado; the mayors of Denver, Colorado and Kansas City, Missouri; the Rhode Island Auditor General and California State Auditor; and the President of the Netherlands Court of Audit.

At the regional level, intergovernmental audit forums around the United States have highlighted key examples of collaboration between audit offices. Several local audit organisations convened at the Pacific Northwest Intergovernmental Audit Forum to discuss ways to audit rental assistance to low-income households in March 2014. Later in 2014, a joint meeting held by three regional intergovernmental audit forums (Mid-America, Southeastern, and Southwest) highlighted the study's planned methodology with a panel featuring GAO and auditing leaders from Oregon and the city and county of Denver. In this study, GAO partnered with 25 state and local audit offices to design an audit plan that six participating audit offices conducted on rental assistance to low-income households. GAO assessed the completed results, reviewed documentation, and interviewed officials from relevant US federal agencies. The resulting GAO report: 1) identified the federal, state, and local government funded programmes that provide rental assistance to low-income households and identifies indications of programme fragmentation and overlap; 2) assessed the extent of intergovernmental collaboration for rental assistance; and 3) determined what is known about performance at the federal level, at selected state and local jurisdictions and for the collective performance of the levels of government providing rental assistance.[13] This report was subsequently discussed at a meeting of the Mid-America Intergovernmental Audit Forum. The Washington State Auditor's Office; the Office of the Multnomah County Auditor in Portland, Oregon; and the City and County of Denver Office of the Auditor also published separate audit reports on low-income rental assistance.

Regional meetings have provided in-depth audit training on GAO's Standards for Internal Controls for the Federal Government (known as the "Green Book") and the Federal Information System Controls Audit Manual (FISCAM). Speakers for regional forums also are drawn from the public sector accountability community at all levels of government and feature individuals from other sectors as well.

The National Intergovernmental Audit Forum Strategic Plan 2014-20 provides a vision for the future that specifies the National Forum's mission, strategic goals and core values. Three strategic goals address the core values of collaboration, professionalism and integrity: 1) fostering networking, dialogue and collaboration on current and emerging issues of common interest within the accountability community; 2) enhancing the capability, credibility, capacity, effectiveness and professionalism of audit organisations by advancing audit standards, sharing best practices and emphasising the importance of accountability within government and the audit profession; and 3) improving the National Forum's outreach, management and impact to assist members in transforming government operations. The National Forum Strategic Plan contains specific measures to evaluate performance such as progress made in monitoring key national trends and initiatives to identify and communicate current and emerging issues and incorporating topics related to best practices in future meeting agendas (National Intergovernmental Audit Forum, 2014). The Plan also references important trends that can shape future efforts, such as: fiscal sustainability, security, governance and interdependence, human capital, effective accountability, technology, and environment and energy.

Annex 2.A2

Accountability and auditing at the state level

In order to gain insights from select Mexican state audit institutions, OECD carried out interviews and circulated a questionnaire in Coahuila, Puebla and Querétaro. This annex provides an overview of these audit institutions and the challenges they face.

Coahuila (Auditoría Superior del Estado de Coahuila, or ASEC)

The Law for Superior Audit and Accountability of the State of Coahuila (Ley de Rendición de Cuentas y Fiscalización Superior del Estado de Coahuila de Zaragoza), which passed into law in November 2014, established the ASEC as a legal body, and provides for technical, management and budgetary autonomy to carry out its functions. ASEC can determine damages to the public accounts and assets of the state government, establish indemnities and economic sanctions, and refer cases of potential criminal wrongdoing to the Attorney's Office for sanctioning. The Superior Auditor is responsible for denouncing criminal activity by public officials. The Superior Auditor also issues internal bylaws of the ASEC, as well as organisation and procedural manuals necessary for its operation. The ASEC annual report should be submitted to the State Congress on 15 December of the year following the audit. The annual report should also be published on ASEC's website on the same date it is submitted to Congress.

Coahuila's Constitution states the Superior Auditor is elected from three candidates selected by the Commission of Finance and Public Accounts by a vote of two-thirds of state representatives and can only be removed through the procedures established in the code of conduct for state and municipal public officials. Reasons for removal include the following:

- removing, destroying, hiding, disclosing or misusing documents or information under his/her custody
- failing to sanction cases as established by law, as well as failing to denounce public officials implicated through audit
- absence for more than a month without authorisation by Congress
- failure to submit the annual report without justification
- participation of third parties in audit work or not acting impartially
- legal incapacity to exercise his duties
- acting under external influence or in regard to his/her personal interests, as well as hiring independent professionals to audit public accounts.

The law also establishes that the Superior Auditor will not be punished because of opinions issued as a result of his/her work, or for recommendations and resolutions. Coahuila's Law for Superior Audit and Accountability was designed in collaboration with IMCO and CUCEA and therefore these institutions' internal bylaws, determination of damages, procedures to allocate responsibilities, and publication of the annual report are not subject to Congressional oversight. The ASEC has budgetary autonomy and the Superior Auditor has the responsibility of presenting the budget proposal to Congress. The budget has increased an average of 7.6% per year from 2011-15 (see Table 2.A2.1).

Table 2.A2.1. **ASEC's budget, 2011-15**

Year	Budget (MXN)	% change
2015	108 895 000	-3.0
2014	112 295 000	16.8
2013	96 183 000	13.5
2012	84 760 000	3.1
2011	82 228 000	N/A

Source: Information provided by ASEC.

Concerning the number of administrative sanctions imposed on public officials, 22 fines were issued in 2013 and a further 22 in 2014 for lack of compliance.

Despite progress, ASEC still has several opportunities to improve, particularly concerning effectiveness and timeliness of sanctions. In the follow-up report to public accounts in 2014, published on 26 January 2016, the ESFE reports no criminal charges were brought because the prosecutor was still analysing recommendations in the original report. As a result, EFSE could not start the process of recovering damages (*responsabilidades resarcitorias*).

In November 2015, 82 notices of administrative responsibilities were issued. Of the 82, 37 correspond to compliance audit and 45 to financial audit. Of those 45, only 16 audited entities responded and initiated procedures for administrative responsibilities within the mandated timeframe (ASEC, 2015).

Puebla (Auditoría Superior del Estado de Puebla, or ASEP)

The Law for Superior Audit and Accountability of the State of Puebla (Ley de Fiscalización Superior y Rendición de Cuentas del Estado de Puebla), passed on 5 February 2015, established the ASEP as the audit, control, and evaluation unit, accountable to the State Congress, with technical and management autonomy to carry out its functions and make decisions regarding its internal structure, functioning, and resolutions.

The ASEP has the power to directly sanction public servants, as well as to determine damages to the public accounts of the state and its municipalities, the federal government where applicable, and the assets of other audited entities. Likewise, it can determine the recovery of damages. It can also seek criminal sanctions and submit the case to the Attorney General. Further, it does require the approval of Congress to initiate the process of administrative sanctioning for public servants.

The Superior Auditor can establish internal bylaws of the ASEP. The ASEP annual report should be submitted to the state congress 12 months after the submission of the public accounts. There is no requirement in the state law to publicise the annual report, however it can be accessed upon request. According to state law, the Superior Auditor is elected by a vote of two-thirds of the state representatives from three candidates proposed by the Governing Board (*Órgano de Gobierno*) of the State Congress. The Superior Auditor can only be removed by a political judgement (*juicio político*) for reasons established in Puebla's Constitution. Such reasons include:

- serious violations of the State Constitution
- irregular management of public funds and resources
- actions or omissions negatively affecting the public interest.

Puebla's Law for Superior Audit and Accountability also has notable weaknesses hindering ASEP's independence. The internal bylaws and the determination of damages are not subject to Congressional oversight, but its approval is needed to initiate the process of administrative responsibilities. Furthermore, the publication of the annual report is not mandatory, despite the fact that the Anticorruption Constitutional Reform makes this an obligation of all EFSEs. Further, the grounds for removing the Superior Auditor are explicit, could be made more specific. The law does not require the development of a professional audit service. In addition, Congress is not legally obligated to use the audit results in the budget process.

The Superior Auditor can however present ASEP's budget proposal to Congress. Its budget has been increasing since 2012, at an average rate of 2.7% from 2011-15 (see Table 2.A2.2). The state law establishes that ASEP's budget will not be less than the budget of the previous year, in order to prevent potential political retaliation by Congress.

Table 2.A2.2. **ASEP's budget, 2011-15**

Year	Budget (MXN)	% change
2015	138 587 971	0
2014	138 587 971	10.2
2013	125 752 580	4.9
2012	119 910 426	-4.5
2011	125 512 726	N/A

Source: Information provided by ASEP.

Concerning the number of administrative sanctions imposed on public officials, 411 fines were issued in 2014 on municipalities, state enterprises, and water management systems for lack of compliance with legal requirements. Likewise, nine disqualifications for public service were imposed in 2014 on seven municipalities, a technical institute, and a water management system. In addition, disqualifications and fines were imposed on 16 municipalities and a water management system. No administrative sanction is recorded for public official of the central administration of the state government.

Querétaro (Entidad Superior de Fiscalización del Estado de Querétaro, or ESFEQ)

The Law for Superior Audit and Accountability of the State of Queretaro (Ley de Fiscalización Superior y Rendición de Cuentas del Estado de Querétaro), published on

December 2014, established that the EFSEQ is an independent body, with technical and management autonomy to make decisions regarding its internal structure, functioning, and resolutions. The EFSEQ has the power to determine damages to the public accounts of the audited entities and directly issue indemnities on responsible officials. It also requires the approval of Congress to launch criminal procedures with the Attorney General. The Superior Auditor has the power to issue the internal bylaws of the EFSEQ, as well as organisational and procedural manuals necessary for its operation.

The ESFEQ annual report should be submitted to the State Congress 270 days after receiving the public accounts.[14] The annual reports remain confidential until analysis and resolution by Congress. Currently audit reports are available for years 2006 to 2013.[15] The Superior Auditor is elected by a vote of two-thirds of the state representatives and can only be removed by specific reasons established by law. Such reasons include the following:

- being a member of a political party or engaging in partisanship
- holding another job or position in the public, private, or social sectors, except for those non-remunerated
- disseminating confidential information under his tenure
- using confidential documents or information for his/her own benefit or that of third parties
- absence for more than a month without authorisation by Congress
- failing to submit the annual report without justification
- removing, hiding, or misusing documents or information in his/her custody
- allowing the influence of political parties in his/her work and acting partially.

Queretaro's Law for Superior Audit and Accountability establishes autonomy to the EFSEQ. Still, there is room for improvement. Congressional approval is needed to initiate criminal proceedings. Further, they cannot publish annual reports at the same time they are submitted to Congress. The law does not require the development of a professional audit service.

Grounds for removal of the Superior Auditor are explicit, however, which protects them from political pressures. The Superior Auditor also presents EFSEQ's budget proposal to Congress, and the EFSEQ can spend the approved budget autonomously. The budget has increased an average of 7.4% per year from 2011-15 (see Table 2.A2.3).

Table 2.A2.3. **ESFEQ's budget, 2011-15**

Year	Budget (MXN)	% change
2015	74 498 640	8.4
2014	68 728 000	8.3
2013	63 438 640	8.6
2012	58 441 509	4.2
2011	56 068 580	N/A

Source: Information provided by ESFEQ.

Notes

1. In addition, collaboration and co-ordination can occur "outwards" with non-government stakeholders, such as civil society and the private sector.

2. Autonomy, as well as other features, was ranked based on 35 indicators. The scale is from 0 to 10, where 10 is the best possible score. As the indicators were built based on state laws in effect until December 2012, the results should be considered with caution, as many of these laws have already been amended. With regard to autonomy, the survey asked the following questions: 1) Does the law for supreme audit institutions reaffirm and develop full autonomy established in the state constitution? (Technical, managerial, organisational, functional and operational); and 2) Are there provisions in the law enforcement or the organic act of the legislature that contradict or substantially limit autonomy?

3. Article 42 of the General Law for the National Anti-Corruption System notes that SNF members should standardise processes, procedures, techniques, criteria strategies, programmes and professional standards in auditing and oversight.

4. The SCII is based on the Standard Model of Internal Control (Modelo Estándar de Control Interno, or MECI), Institutional Risk Management (Administración de Riesgos Institucionales, or ARI) and the Institutional Development and Control Committee (Comité de Control y Desempeño Institucional, or COCODI).

5. The Auditor General of Canada is also the Auditor General for the three territories – Nunavut, the Northwest Territories and the Yukon.

6. In addition to voting rights, Associate Members are required to contribute to the CCOLA budget, whereas Observer Members are not.

7. A list of the Federal Inspectors General may be found at www.ignet.gov/content/inspectors-general-directory

8. The United States is made up of 50 states and 6 territories (American Samoa, District of Columbia, Guam, Northern Marianas Islands, Puerto Rico, and US Virgin Islands).

9. The National Forum also provides information relevant to private sector auditors who audit federally funded programmes and academic, industry and non-profit organisations.

10. These were the Council of State Governments, the Municipal Finance Officers Association (now the Government Finance Officers Association) and other agencies and organisations.

11. "Standards for Audit of Governmental Organizations, Programs, Activities and Functions", now known as the "Generally Accepted Government Auditing Standards". For more information, see www.gao.gov/yellowbook/overview.

12. "A Framework for Managing Fraud Risks in Federal Programs", GAO-15-593SP, 28 July 2015. For more information, see http://gao.gov/products/GAO-15-593SP.

13. "Affordable Rental Housing: Assistance is Provided by Federal, State, and Local Programs, but There is Incomplete Information on Collective Performance", GAO-15-645. For more information, see www.gao.gov/products/GAO-15-645.

14. Public accounts should be submitted to the State Congress, via the ESFEQ, on the last day of February of the following year to the one being audited, at the latest.

15. Review conducted on 7 March 2016.

References

ANAO (Australian National Audit Office) (2012), "Public Sector Internal Audit", Better Practice Guide, September, www.anao.gov.au/sites/g/files/net616/f/2012_Public_Sector_Internal_Audit.pdf.

ASEC (Auditoría Superior del Estado de Coahuila) (2015), "Informe de Seguimiento 2014", www.asecoahuila.gob.mx/actualizacion/PDF/IS_2014.pdf (accessed 1 March 2016).

ASF (Auditoria Superior de la Federación) (2015), "The Basis for Operations" [Bases Operativas para el Funcionamiento del SNF], published on 22 July 2015, www.snf.org.mx/bases-operativas-para-el-funcionamiento-del-snf-1.aspx.

ASOFIS (Asociación Nacional de Organismos de Fiscalización Superior y Control Gubernamental) (2016), *Antecedentes*, database, www.asofis-basededatos.org.mx/.

Centre for Public Finances of the Mexican Chamber of Deputies (2015), "Informative Note on Subnational Spending", January, www.cefp.gob.mx/publicaciones/nota/2015/enero/notacefp0032015.pdf (accessed 7 July 2016).

Charbit, C. and M. Michalun (2009), "Mind the gaps: Managing mutual dependence in relations among levels of government", *OECD Working Papers on Public Governance*, No. 14, OECD Publishing, Paris, http://dx.doi.org/10.1787/221253707200.

European Union (2014), "Compendium of the public internal control systems in the EU Member States", http://ec.europa.eu/budget/pic/lib/book/compendium/HTML/index.html.

European Union (2012), "Compendium of the public internal control systems in the EU Member States", http://ec.europa.eu/budget/library/biblio/publications/2011/compendium_27_countries_en.pdf.

EUROSAI-ECIIA (2014), "Co-ordination and Co-operation between Supreme Audit Institutions and Internal Auditors in the Public Sector", joint paper, www.eciia.eu/wp-content/uploads/2014/05/EUROSAI_ECIIA_Joint_Paper_05052014.pdf.

FERMA-ECIIA (2014), "Guidance on the 8th EU Company Law Directive", www.ferma.eu/about/publications/eciia-ferma-guidance/.

GAO (Government Accountability Office) (2014), "Standards for Internal Control in the Federal Government", www.gao.gov/products/GAO-14-704G.

GAO (1996), "Single Audit Refinements Can Improve Usefulness", GAO/T-AIMD-96-77, March.

Government of Canada (2015), "Policy on Transfer Payments", www.tbs-sct.gc.ca/pol/doc-eng.aspx?id=13525.

Government of Canada (2010), "Guideline on Recipient Audits Under the Policy on Transfer Payments and the Directive on Transfer Payments", www.tbs-sct.gc.ca/pol/doc-eng.aspx?id=19061#fn18.

Government of New Zealand (2016), "Part 1: Financial reporting in the public sector and why it matters", Controller and Auditor-General New Zealand, 24 February, www.oag.govt.nz/2016/financial-reporting/part1.htm?searchterm=purpose+reports.

IMCO (Mexican Institute for Competitiveness) and CUCEA (Centre for Economic and Administrative Sciences of the University of Guadalajara) (2013), "Auditorías Superiores Locales en México: Evaluación de su Normatividad, Prácticas y Transparencia", http://rendiciondecuentas.org.mx/wp-content/uploads/2013/05/Reporte_completo_IMCO-UDG.pdf (accessed 2 March 2016).

INTOSAI (International Organisation of Supreme Audit Institutions) (2010a), "Guidelines for Internal Control Standards for the Public Sector", www.issai.org/media/13329/intosai_gov_9100_e.pdf.

INTOSAI (2010b), "Internal Audit Independence in the Public Sector", www.issai.org/media/13349/intosai_gov_9140_e_.pdf

INTOSAI (2007a), "Mexico Declaration on SAI Independence", *International Standards of Supreme Audit Institutions* (ISSAI), 11, INTOSAI Professional Standard Committee Secretariat, Copenhagen, www.issai.org.

INTOSAI (2007b), "Building capacity in supreme audit institutions: A guide", INTOSAI Capacity Building Committee, www.intosaicbc.org/mdocs-posts/buildingcapacity insaisguide_englishversion/.

INTOSAI (2004), "GOV 9100 Guidelines for Internal Control Standards for the Public Sector", www.intosai.org/issai-executive-summaries/view/article/intosai-gov-9100-guidelinesfor-internal-control-standards-for-the-public-sector.html.

INTOSAI (2001), "GOV 9120 Internal Control: Providing a Foundation for Accountability in Government", www.issai.org/media/13337/intosai_gov_9120_e.pdf.

INTOSAI (1977), "Lima Declaration of Guidelines on Auditing Precepts", *International Standards of Supreme Audit Institutions* (ISSAI), 1, INTOSAI Professional Standard Committee Secretariat, Copenhagen, www.issai.org.

National Intergovernmental Audit Forum (2016), "Regional audit fórums", webpage, http://auditforum.org/about-us/regional-audit-forums/ (accessed 23 June 2016).

National Intergovernmental Audit Forum (2014), "National Intergovernmental Audit Forum Draft Strategic Plan, 2014–2020", https://iaftestzone.files.wordpress.com/2015/10/niaf-sp-10-5-2015-v11-web1.pdf (accessed 18 September 2016).

OECD (2016), *Supreme Audit Institutions and Good Governance: Oversight, Insight and Foresight*, OECD Publishing, Paris, http://dx.doi.org/10.1787/9789264263871-en.

OECD (2014), *Regulatory Policy in Mexico: Towards a Whole-of-Government Perspective to Regulatory Improvement*, OECD Publishing, Paris, http://dx.doi.org/10.1787/9789264203389-en.

OECD (2013), *OECD Economic Surveys: Mexico 2013*, OECD Publishing, Paris, http://dx.doi.org/10.1787/eco_surveys-mex-2013-en.

OMB (Office of Management and Budget) (2015), "Circular A-133 Compliance Supplement 2015", www.whitehouse.gov/omb/circulars/a133_compliance_supplement_2015.

OMB (2009), "Management's Responsibility for Internal Control", Circular A-123, www.whitehouse.gov/sites/default/files/omb/assets/agencyinformation_circulars_pdf/a123_appendix_b.pdf.

OMB (n.d.), "Office of Federal Financial Management Single Audit", webpage, www.whitehouse.gov/omb/financial_fin_single_audit (accessed 18 September 2016).

Papadopoulos, Yannie (2008), "Accountability and Multi-Level Governance: More Accountability, Less Democracy?", Institut d'Etudes Politiques et Internationales, University of Lausanne, http://paperroom.ipsa.org/papers/paper_2873.pdf.

PEMEX (Petróleos Mexicanos) (2015), "Macro de Administracion de Riesgo Empresariales", presentation, 25 November.

Santiso, Carlos (2007), "Eyes wide shut? The politics of autonomous audit agencies in emerging economies", Centro de Implementación de Políticas Públicas para la Equidad y el Crecimiento.

SNF (Sistema Nacional de Fiscalización) (2015), "Strategic Plan for 2013-2017", published October 2012, www.snf.org.mx/SharedFiles/Download.aspx?pageid=52&mid=93&fileid=8.

SNF (2014), "Normas Profesionales de Auditoría de Sistema Nacional de Fiscalización", SNF Publishing, www.snf.org.mx/normas-profesionales-1.aspx.

Chapter 3

Mexico's supreme audit institution as a catalyst for better governance

This chapter proposes actions for Mexico's supreme audit institution (the Auditoria Superior de la Federación, or ASF) and Congress to ensure the effectiveness of new auditing authorities and enhance the contributions of audits for improved governance. This chapter offers insights for ASF to capitalise on its strengths and identifies opportunities to improve the impact of auditing on governance in Mexico, including proposals for government-wide reviews of key issues, integrating new audit authorities strategically and improving ASF's outreach to external stakeholders. Moreover, the effectiveness of Mexico's National Auditing System (Sistema Nacional de Fiscalización, or SNF) relies not only on ASF, but also on Congress as a key user of ASF's audit reports. This chapter explores ways for Congress to better deliver on its own responsibilities for accountability in Mexico, such as improving its capacity to use ASF's audit work to inform laws, budgets and oversight.

Introduction

Mexico's supreme audit institution (SAI), the Auditoria Superior de la Federación (ASF), plays a vital role in government given its overarching view of the governance arrangements. SAIs are not only critical for oversight, as commonly known, but they also provide insight and foresight by working across the executive and legislative branches to improve policy making (OECD, 2016). In this way, SAIs can help to improve governance by contributing audits and evaluations of systemic, government-wide issues across the policy cycle.

Recent reforms, like greater latitude for ASF in audit planning and additional reporting requirements to Congress throughout the fiscal year, aim to enhance the relevance of ASF's work for users, particularly Congress. For these reforms to be fully effective, both ASF and Congress can consider ways to address challenges that limit the uptake of ASF's work in Congress and among audited entities. For ASF, this could include internal changes to improve the quality and level of external engagement by Congress and citizenry. Similarly, opportunities exist for Congress itself to review its own role in the system, and make improvements to strengthen accountability and governance to improve the lives of Mexico's citizens.

This chapter explores these challenges and proposes actions for ASF and Congress to ensure the effectiveness of new auditing authorities and enhance the contributions of audits for improved governance. ASF, as a leader within the National Auditing System (Sistema Nacional de Fiscalización, or SNF) and others systems, will have many responsibilities that will affect its mission, strategy, operations, audit portfolio and interactions with external stakeholders. ASF could take a number of actions to position itself for success amid constitutional changes and a new auditing environment. Table 3.1 summarises the proposals for action addressed in this chapter.

Table 3.1. **Proposals for action for Mexico's supreme audit institution (ASF) and Congress to ensure the effectiveness of new auditing authorities**

Improving governance through audits of systemic issues	ASF could apply its comparative advantage in auditing to lead government-wide studies and audits of the implementation of the National Transparency System's strategy to strengthen transparency.
	ASF could conduct, to complement its forensic audits and investigations, evaluations of systemic deficiencies in internal control and risk management to improve broader governance functions.
Integrating ASF's new auditing authorities strategically for greater impact and relevance	ASF could help ensure the timeliness and uptake of its work in Congress by effectively aligning its new authorities, such as early audit planning and conducting real-time audits, with its traditional audit programming.
	ASF could focus its audits early in the fiscal year on high-risk programmes, as well as programme performance, in order to increase the value of reports for the budgetary decision-making process.
Strengthening accountability by improving the uptake of ASF's audits	Congress could build its own technical capacity in order to increase uptake of inputs from ASF and the SNF.
	ASF could assess its internal quality-control processes in order to ensure the relevance and quality of its products for Congress amid additional reporting requirements.
	ASF and state audit institutions could enhance outreach, communication strategies and trainings to improve the relevance and impact of their work among key stakeholders, including Congress, its committees, auditees and citizens.

Improving governance through audits of systemic issues

ASF could apply its comparative advantage in auditing to lead government-wide studies and audits of the implementation of the National Transparency System's strategy to strengthen transparency.

ASF holds a unique position in government given its authority to collect information from public agencies and other actors. Unlike other institutions in the National Auditing System (Sistema Nacional de Fiscalización, or SNF), ASF will have a formal role as a member of the National Transparency System (Sistema Nacional de Transparencia, Acceso a la Información y Protección de Datos Personales, or SNT), and will therefore have additional responsibilities to promote transparency within a new system. Moreover, as Mexico's supreme audit institution, ASF's mandate is much broader than other audit institutions in that its purview for external control reaches across government at federal and state levels. ASF's responsibilities as part of the SNT suggest the need for further consideration about how it can leverage this mandate and expertise, and the comparative advantages that come with it, to strengthen transparency through its auditing work.

The Law on the Accountability and Submission of the Accounts of the Federation (Ley de Fiscalización y Rendición de Cuentas de la Federación, or LFRCF) grants ASF the power to request and obtain information for the completion of its work. ASF also can access confidential and secret information related to the management of federal revenues, expenditures, and public debt. ASF must maintain the same level of confidentiality, including limiting disclosure of confidential or secret information in its report, whether obtained from government or financial firms (LFRCF, Article 17). ASF may also approach public and private persons that have a relationship with audited entities, as needed, and can access any information that may be needed to perform auditing tasks if the request identifies the objectives in using such information (ASF, 2013).

ASF's legal authority to access information and data within and outside of government, coupled with its audit expertise and knowledge to analyse what it collects, is its comparative advantage in the SNT. ASF could consider how it can leverage this advantage to contribute to the broader goals of the SNT and the coherence of transparency policies, while avoiding overextending itself in the SNT. The experience of other SAIs is instructive. As noted in Box 3.1, many SAIs are directing audit resources to government-wide reviews of transparency initiatives.

Box 3.1. Supreme audit institutions conducting government-wide auditing for greater transparency

In a recent study, OECD reviewed the contributions of ten supreme audit institutions (SAIs) to the policy cycle and its outcomes. The participating SAIs represented Brazil, Canada, Chile, France, Korea, Netherlands, Poland, Portugal, South Africa and the United States. The report highlighted that delivering value for money is a shared goal between the Legislature, the Executive and SAIs, leveraging all actors' potential. SAIs provide insight to reduce duplication, fragmentation and overlap in government, and foresight to help government understand long-term policy challenges and risks, such as climate and demographic change. In addition, SAIs are carrying out cross-cutting work to understand the effectiveness of transparency and information-sharing efforts across government (see examples below), such as audits and evaluations of the following areas:

Box 3.1. **Supreme audit institutions conducting government-wide auditing for greater transparency** *(continued)*

- openness of government-wide strategic planning processes
- openness of budgetary planning processes, including the existence and adequacy of participative debates on budgetary choices
- openness and consultation of regulatory policy processes
- compliance with freedom-of-information laws.

The following are examples from countries conducting government-wide reviews of initiatives to promote the principles of transparency.

Brazil

The Tribunal de Contas da União (TCU) undertook a survey and issued a report on data openness in the federal government. The TCU proposed solutions on collection, storage and processing of big data, in order to enhance transparency and modernise public management (TCU, 2014).

Korea

The Board of Audit and Inspection (BAI) conducted an audit on the status of public information sharing connected to a national information system for increasing government efficiency. BAI found a lack of public information sharing by individual authorities hindered the rollout of information technology systems, and hampered the appropriate use of existing information (BAI, 2013).

United Kingdom

The National Audit Office (NAO) conducted a cross-government review in 2012 titled, "Implementing Transparency," which assessed the progress of the Cabinet Office and other bodies in the Executive Branch to implement a sweeping transparency agenda. This government-wide review resulted in a number of practical findings, such as the need for an evaluative framework to measure the value for money of transparency efforts, and further actions to ensure the quality and usability of government data.

United States

The Government Accountability Office's "Federal Rulemaking: Regulatory Review Processes Could Be Enhanced" (2014) underlined the importance of oversight by the executive in formulating and co-ordinating regulatory policies to foster more coherence across government. It recommends greater transparency and increased openness of rule-making procedures as well as the implementation of more streamlined regulations.

Source: OECD (2016), *Supreme Audit Institutions and Good Governance: Oversight, Insight and Foresight*, OECD Publishing, Paris, http://dx.doi.org/10.1787/9789264263871-en; TCU (2014) "Open data: A strategy for increased public management transparency and modernization", *Revista do TCU*, September/December 2014, http://revista.tcu.gov.br/ojs/index.php/RTCU/article/viewFile/59/324; BAI (2013), "Audit on the status of public information sharing", ' 25 July, http://bai.go.kr/cmm/fdm/FileDown.do?atchFileId=20130725140023518&fileSn=1&siteId=bai&bbsId=BBSMSTR_100000000009; NAO (2012), "Cross government review: Implementing transparency", report by the Comptroller and Auditor General, HC 1833 Session 2010-2012, www.nao.org.uk/wp-content/uploads/2012/04/10121833.pdf.

Government-wide reviews like those described in Box 3.1 are similar to those ASF has conducted related to integrity and anti-corruption measures across government (see Box 3.2). Such reviews can also involve state-level audit institutions in co-ordinated approaches to reviewing the implementation of programmes at all levels of government, as discussed in Chapter 2. However, in conducting such work, ASF could consider the extent to which its independence could be compromised by its involvement in the SNT. ASF's role in the SNT is still under consideration; however, the system as a whole is responsible for an array of activities, including the design and implementation of transparency policies and mechanisms in government. In defining its involvement in the SNT and potential reviews regarding these activities, ASF should take steps to maintain its independence in accordance with international standards for supreme audit institutions, as noted in Chapter 2.

Box 3.2. **Mexico's supreme audit institution and government-wide studies for improved integrity systems**

Institutional mechanisms, policy interactions, contextual factors and effects are all examples of elements that contribute to policy coherence (OECD, 2015). SAIs are in a unique position to look across government agencies to assess an issue and the extent to which governments are achieving policy and operational coherence. For instance, they offer perspectives of oversight, insight and foresight to reviews of policies and programme planning, such as the integration of government-wide objectives into current strategies and planning and the preparedness of government to tackle future goals.

Every year since 2012, ASF has conducted at least one government-wide integrity review that touches on elements of coherence, looking specifically at the strategies and mechanisms of federal public institutions to strengthen integrity and prevent corruption. These studies focus on what government is doing in these areas, particularly activities related to internal control systems and risk-management functions. Examples of these studies include the following:

- *General Study of the Conditions of the Institutional Internal Control System in the Federal Public Sector* – ASF conducted a study of 279 institutions in the executive branch, in addition to approximately a dozen entities of the legislature, judiciary and autonomous constitutional bodies, to compare internal control frameworks based on standards of the Committee of Sponsoring Organisations of the Treadway Commission. The study aimed to compare internal control frameworks in these entities and identify opportunities for improvements (ASF, 2012).
- *Continuation to the Studies of Internal Control and the Diffusion of the Study of Integrity in the Public Sector* – ASF conducted this study to determine the progress that the federal public sector institutions had had on the implementation of strategies it suggested for strengthening internal control, and to continue promoting the establishment of a culture of integrity (ASF, 2013).
- *Study about the Strategies for Combating Corruption in the Public Sector* – ASF conducted this study to understand the actions federal public sector institutions had been making to tackle corruption, based on the applicable standards and international best practices, in order to identify areas of opportunity and promote the implementation of an integrity programme (ASF, 2014).
- *Technical Study for the Promotion of a Culture of Integrity in the Public Sector* - ASF analysed and described the best international practices in integrity, as well as implementation of anti-corruption controls, to help government institutions formulate an integrity programme for strengthening the culture of transparency, probity and accountability (ASF, 2015a).

Source: ASF (2012), "General Study of the Conditions of the Institutional Internal Control System in the Federal Public Sector", http://asf.gob.mx/uploads/180_Estudios/1172_Estudio_General_de_la_Situacion_que_Guarda_el_Sistema_de_Control_Interno_Institucional_en_el_Sector_Publico_Federal.pdf; ASF (2013), "Continuation to the Studies of Internal Control and the Diffusion of the Study of Integrity in the Public Sector", http://asf.gob.mx/uploads/180_Estudios/1198_Continuidad_a_los_Estudios_de_Control_Interno_y_a_la_Difusion_del_Estudio_de_Integridad_en_el_Sector_Publico.pdf; ASF (2014), "Study about the Strategies for Combating Corruption in the Public Sector", http://informe.asf.gob.mx/Documentos/Auditorias/2014_1642_a.pdf; ASF (2015a), "Technical Study for the Promotion of a Culture of Integrity in the Public Sector", http://asf.gob.mx/uploads/180_Estudios/1173_Estudio_Tec_para_la_Promocion_de_la_Cultura_de_Integridad_en_el_Sec_Pub.pdf.

ASF could conduct, to complement its forensic audits and investigations, evaluations of systemic deficiencies in internal control and risk management to improve broader governance functions.

The comparative advantage of an SAI, in relation to other actors in an accountability system, is its knowledge and experience in providing independent oversight, insight, and foresight through its auditing and evaluation work. As noted in Chapter 1, recent reforms and legislation grant ASF the authority to conduct investigations relating to "grave" administrative irregularities and to substantiate cases. The units responsible for these duties would be independent from each other, but also independent from ASF's ongoing forensic audit work. ASF officials also said ASF will support criminal cases, which generally fall under the jurisdiction of the Special Prosecutor for Anti-Corruption, with information and evidence obtained during the course of its forensic audits. Chapter 1 emphasised various strategic considerations for ASF to effectively implement these new authorities, highlighting various risks related to overextension and resource constraints, among others. To help mitigate these risks, ASF could focus on its comparative advantage in auditing and clarify this purpose in its strategic plan and procedures, as discussed in Chapter 1. Building on this proposal, ASF can further leverage its comparative advantage, and complement its new authorities, by investing in its forensic audit work and reviews of systemic issues.

ASF conducts forensic audits within its Special Financial Compliance Auditor Division and under the leadership of the Director General of Forensic Audits (DGFA). ASF established the DGFA in 2009 to combat fraud and corruption identified during audits of the year-end account. The Director General of Forensic Audits leads the operational aspects of conducting forensic audits, including the review of processes, facts or evidence for detecting and investigating irregularities or unlawful conduct (ASF, 2014). As of early 2016, the DGFA had a team of approximately 55 directors, subdirectors and auditors. The DGFA team consists of forensic experts, lawyers, accountants, public administrators, as well as information technology specialists, who staff a forensic lab for analysing fraud and corruption cases. ASF's forensic audits come primarily from two sources, including indications of wrongdoing identified during audits of public account, as well as individual complaints. In 2015 (for fiscal year 2014), less than 1% (10) of all audits ASF conducted (1 648) were forensic audits (ASF, 2015b).[1] Of the 63 forensic audits ASF has conducted since 2010, 129 cases have been filed and 1 resulted in a warrant for arrest, while the remaining 128 cases are still ongoing.

ASF officials said the purpose of their forensic audits is not to examine breakdowns in internal controls or risk management within the government entity, but rather to assess potential wrongdoing related to individual cases. This case-by-case approach is partly based on what officials see as a division of responsibilities between ASF and SFP, which is the entity with the primary mandate for ensuring the effectiveness of internal control systems in government. Presently, ASF considers the effectiveness of systems on an ad hoc basis. ASF could enhance its contributions to good governance by strategically and systematically considering, during the course of its forensic audits, the systemic internal control and risk-management problems an entity is facing. For instance, ASF could incorporate specific research objectives into its forensic audit planning that helps to guide teams in identifying the root causes of specific cases of potential fraud or corruption, including breakdowns in the internal control and risk-management systems. Such an objective could also be considered during investigations as an *ex post* exercise that would help ASF to go beyond a case-by-case approach.

Complementing individual investigations with assessments of internal control and risk-management deficiencies could help ASF to differentiate itself from other actors as a change agent for better governance. As discussed, ASF's comparative advantage is in its auditing expertise, its government-wide view and authority to make recommendations to the Executive Branch for taking corrective actions. Moreover, in general, the strengths of an SAI in a system to promote accountability is not necessarily to lead investigations, but rather to provide investigative support. Some SAIs have investigative units; however, SAIs generally tend not to lead investigations, since they often do not possess the adequate knowledge or resources to do so (INTOSAI, 2013a). Investigative authorities may even ask the SAI to stop carrying out audit work in the area concerned so as not to jeopardise the findings of the investigation team. Alternatively, the SAI may also be asked to co-operate and even work alongside the investigative team (INTOSAI, 2013a).

In support of investigations, SAIs often provide analysis of financial accounts, databases and documentation, using methodologies like database matching and data mining (see Box 3.3) to identify patterns or instances of potential wrongdoing. As ASF itself notes in its strategy for 2011 to 2017, "detection and prevention of corrupt practices is not a central task of the audit function, and ASF should provide, in the area of its competence, 'elements' to help reduce the recurrence of such practices in public administration by pointing to areas prone to excess opacity and discretion (ASF, 2011).

Box 3.3. Data analytics and techniques for enhanced auditing of integrity and performance

Rapid digitalisation has led to mass generation and preservation of meaningful data. Supreme audit institutions, given their mandate and legal authority to access data, have significant opportunities to leverage both open data and public sector information (see Chapter 1) to greatly enhance their capacities and audit work. For instance, the Netherlands Court of Audits is unique in that it is the only Dutch institution that can access sensitive and confidential information, both public and private, such as data of the Dutch secret service, Tax Office and Ministry of Defence (Janssen, 2016). Many SAIs do not enjoy such access. Nonetheless, opportunities exist for SAIs to make use of the data they can obtain and analyse to investigate potential fraud and corruption, conduct performance audits and evaluate outcomes, and generally offer insight and foresight about developing trends or systemic issues governments face.

Data analytics, which include various approaches for analysing and understanding data, can be particularly effective in preventing and detecting potential fraud or corruption. One technique, predictive analytics, includes automated systems and tools that can be used to identify particular types of behaviour, including potential fraud, before transactions are complete (GAO, 2015). Predictive models can use historical data to help identify processes associated with known forms of fraud or corruption, and can then apply the models to pending transactions to prevent fraud before it occurs. As indicated, the role of the SAI in this respect is often the identification of *potential* fraud or corruption, as opposed to *actual* wrongdoing, since the latter can be a determination of a responsible adjudicative body, such as an attorney's or prosecutor's office.

Approaches and techniques of data analytics

In addition to predictive analytics, there are also techniques that aim to detect fraud that has already occurred. For instance, script-based analysis inspects mass amounts of data through continuous combinations and comparisons with other data sources in order to identify anomalies. This technique makes it easier to identify root issues and trends. Often lack of scrutiny of all individual transactions enables fraud, as many internal control systems have serious weaknesses that can be exploited (GAO, 2015). Accordingly, data analytics can be particularly effective in transaction-heavy areas, such as expenditures, payroll and accounts payable, billing, and capital projects, further demonstrating its relevance for investigation of fraud and corruption.

Box 3.3. **Data analytics and techniques for enhanced auditing of integrity and performance** *(continued)*

Similarly, data mining and data matching can also be effective techniques for detecting fraud that has already occurred. Data matching is a large-scale comparison of big data that disregards duplicates in order to identify very specific matters of interest. Data mining views large data from different perspectives to extract buried or previously unknown information. For instance, a federal interagency taskforce in Chile, which included representatives from the Council for the Internal Auditor General of Government, recently made use of data mining to prevent fraud and corruption in public procurement. By mining the newly innovated e-procurement transactions, they have been able to avoid bid rigging and break up collusive games among suppliers, officials, and procurement officers (OECD, 2010).

Using data analytics for performance audits in India

In addition to its application for preventing and detecting fraud or corruption, data analytics can also be applied to other areas of SAIs' work. For instance, India's SAI (the Comptroller and Auditor General of India), has actively invested in data analytics and applied it to its audits of the social security programme, which aims to protect citizens, particularly vulnerable populations, from unforeseen circumstances and financial risks. During a performance audit of the social assistance programmes of Old Age Pensions, Widow Pensions and Disabled Pension schemes, the SAI strategically made use of data in its audit model. This was a departure from its conventional approach, which still would have allowed the auditors to detect improper payments to ineligible persons in pension schemes. However, by leveraging more external data than traditional approaches, the auditors were able to verify whether eligible beneficiaries were excluded, resulting in a performance audit that was considerably more thorough and insightful (SAI India, n.d.). In addition, in February 2016, India's SAI established a new Big Data Management Policy, which included a categorisation of data sources into internal (i.e. created and maintained by the SAI) and external (i.e. available from audited entities or is in the public domain). Further, there is a strict protocol to ensure the data is authentic, relevant and useable, among other things, and also sets out guidelines for data access arrangements with external sources. Finally, the India SAI established a monitoring group to oversee the implementation of this sweeping new policy to optimise the potential for new data analytical technology (SAI India, n.d.).

Weighing the benefits and challenges of data analytics

While opportunities exist for SAIs to make better use of data in their audit work, there are also risks that should be considered when employing data analytics. For example, if the analysis of data is not relevant to the audit, not well controlled, is unreliable, or if the source of the information is not well understood, it could have a negative impact on the quality of audit (IAASB, 2016). Thus, while data analytics can lead to valuable insights, it will not provide everything the auditor needs to know and still requires human judgement when interpreting results. Human error when conducting data analytics, as well as errors in the data themselves, highlights challenges SAIs may face in ensuring data is valid, appropriate and reliable for their purposes. In addition, challenges remain for auditors to reconcile data analytics and international auditing standards. For instance, there is speculation over whether analysis of entity data across 100% of a population provides only risk assessment information or whether it also provides substantive audit evidence as well. In risk assessment particularly, auditors will need to consider how much substantive or control evidence needs to be reduced with data from 100% of the population. The types of challenges SAIs can face when employing data analytics will vary, depending on the maturity of the SAI in terms of capacity, expertise and infrastructure, as well as external factors, like the legal framework for accessing and using data (IAASB, 2016). Regardless of the type of challenges, in an increasingly digitised world, SAIs are likely to continue facing pressure to maintain their relevance by modernising this aspect of their activities through changes to strategy, resource allocation, training and audit techniques.

Source: SAI India (n.d.), "Big data analytics in SAI India", a presentation by the Comptroller and Auditor General of India, www.google.fr/url?sa=t&rct=j&q=&esrc=s&source=web&cd=2&ved=0ahUKEwjw18C35MfNAhVB1RoKHaNbBmwQFgg7MAE&url=http%3A%2F%2Fportal.tcu.gov.br%2Flumis%2Fportal%2Ffile%2FfileDownload.jsp%3FfileId%3D8A8182A25454C5A8015469F0E2D42BF5&usg=AFQjCNEZ20zwPPjgl2FUq6acxzJx4VfN_A (accessed 18 September 2016); GAO (2015), "A Framework for Managing Fraud Risks in Federal Programs", July, www.gao.gov/assets/680/671664.pdf; IAASB (2016), "The IAASB's work to explore the growing use of technology in the audit, including data analytics", 21 June, www.iaasb.org/system/files/meetings/files/20160621-IAASB-Agenda_Item_8A-Data-Analytics-Working-Group-Publication-final_0.pdf; Janssen, R. (2016) *The Art of Audit: Eight Remarkable Government Auditors on Stage*, Amsterdam University Press, The Hague; OECD (2010), "Policy Roundtables: Collusion and Corruption in Public Procurement 2010", www.oecd.org/competition/cartels/46235884.pdf.

Outside of Mexico, there are various examples of SAIs that have effectively taken on an investigative support role with an emphasis on identifying systemic control deficiencies (see Box 3.4). In this capacity, SAIs can leverage their comparative advantage in auditing the performance of internal control systems, and when the occasion arises, refer potential cases of fraud or corruption to the relevant law enforcement or prosecutorial bodies. The focus of the SAI then becomes identifying fraud and corruption risks, as opposed to building a case for proving actual fraud or corruption in an individual instance. Such an investigative support role is aligned with leading practices for combating fraud and corruption, which emphasises prevention and well-designed controls over detection, as the latter can be costly and result in a "pay-and-chase" model.

Box 3.4. **Supreme audit institutions that have effectively taken on an investigative support role**

United Kingdom

The UK National Audit Office (NAO) conducts investigations as one dimension of its work. From 2014 to 2015, NAO published 13 investigations in response to important issues facing the government, including the role of prescribed persons in whistleblowing, potential abuse of financial aid at alternative higher education providers and concerns about potential wrongdoing in a company owned by the Minister of State for Health. The investigative work focuses on financial management, better use of information, and other specific areas of interests raised by Members of Parliament or the general public. The NAO's investigative work provides in-depth analysis into the systemic issues faced across government, including the effective use of information and communication technologies, as well as leading practices in financial management.

South Africa

The primary role of the Auditor General of South Africa (AGSA) is to audit and report to Parliament within the areas of compliance and financial auditing. However, in line with international trends and because of increases in fraud and corruption, a small forensic auditing division was established in 1997. The objective of the division is to: 1) determine the nature and extent of "economic crime" as well as the adequacy of measures to prevent and detect it; and 2) facilitate investigations by providing support to relevant investigatory or prosecutorial bodies. To achieve these objectives, AGSA defines a "proactive" and "reactive" strategy. The former includes an emphasis on prevention and review of effective internal controls, recognising that these measures serve as deterrents for would-be perpetrators of economic crime. The reactive strategy consists of actions to facilitate investigations of specific crimes. The forensic auditing division interacts with other agencies in a supportive role for investigations of alleged corruption. The AGSA may also conduct investigations or special audits of institutions if the Auditor General (AG) considers it to be in the public interest or upon the receipt of a complaint or request. It can also investigate a matter raised by a member of the public if the AG considers it to be in the public interest.

Indonesia

In a peer review of the Indonesian Supreme Audit Institution (Badan Pemeriksa Keuangan, BPK), the SAI of Poland highlights forensic audits as a strength of the BPK, noting that law-enforcement agencies value this body of BPK's work as effective support for their investigations. BPK generally categorises forensic audits as "special purpose audits", which are neither financial nor performance audits, and can be triggered by a request from parliament, government, or law-enforcement agencies, or can be carried out on the BPK's own initiative. The special audits are sometimes treated as compliance audits, but they can also be forensic audits and carried out as support for investigations led by law-enforcement agencies.

Source: Supreme Audit Office of Poland (2014), "Peer Review Report on the Supreme Audit Board of the Republic of Indonesia – Badan Pemeriska Keuangan," www.bpk.go.id/assets/files/attachments/attach_page_1399279800.pdf; IAACA (International Association of Anti-Corruption Authorities) (n.d.), "Office of the Auditor General", webpage, www.iaaca.org/AntiCorruptionAuthorities/ByCountriesandRegions/S/SouthAfrica1/201202/t20120215_804900.shtml (accessed April 2016); NAO (n.d.), "Investigations", webpage, www.nao.org.uk/about-us/our-work/investigations/ (accessed April 2016).

Indeed, in Mexico, recent reforms shape a new role for the ASF that goes beyond investigative support, which will require a strategic approach for effective implementation, as discussed in Chapter 1. In addition, given its composition and expertise, the DGFA may have to invest additional resources to bolster its forensic audit work with a broader systemic angle, or it could co-ordinate with other teams within ASF. Various audit teams within ASF identify and report on internal control and risk-management deficiencies among audited entities. The DGFA could take advantage of the experience and expertise across units with sectoral or thematic focus in order to enhance its forensic audits and investigations. This form of co-operation could take multiple forms. For instance, the forensic audit unit could co-ordinate with sectoral teams to identify specific control issues a ministry has historically faced, similar to the model employed by the US Government Accountability Office. The "systemic" nature of such reviews could mean they focus on multiple government entities, or they could consider the ministry or programme level. Such reviews can complement ASF's new investigative work in that individual cases of wrongdoing can serve as powerful, real-world examples to illustrate the actual effect of vulnerabilities in the internal control and risk-management systems.

Integrating ASF's new auditing authorities strategically for greater impact and relevance

ASF could help ensure the timeliness and uptake of its work in Congress by effectively aligning its new authorities, such as early audit planning and real-time audits, with its traditional audit programming.

As one of its primary duties, ASF audits the year-end account of individual government entities, as well as the consolidated government year-end account. The impact of this work hinges in part on the timelines of reporting on audit results. ASF's audit work is currently conducted entirely *ex post*, based on one fiscal year. Moreover, the year-end audit report is submitted to Congress 14 months after the end of the fiscal year. This is more than twice the standard set out in OECD's leading practices for budget transparency, which notes that the year-end report, as the government's key accountability document, should be released within six months of the end of the fiscal year (OECD, 2002). Moreover, international standards note that the audit report should be published and submitted in a manner that is timely, relevant and objective (INTOSAI, 2013b). As a result of current issues with timeliness, ASF's audit findings are not available to inform budget deliberations for the following fiscal year, which lessens the potential for improving financial performance and creating more transparent allocation processes. Figure 3.1 provides a comparison between Mexico and other countries on the completion of the audit of the consolidated year-end government report.

Figure 3.1. **Number of months supreme audit institutions submit year-end audit reports after the end of the fiscal year: Mexico and selected OECD countries**

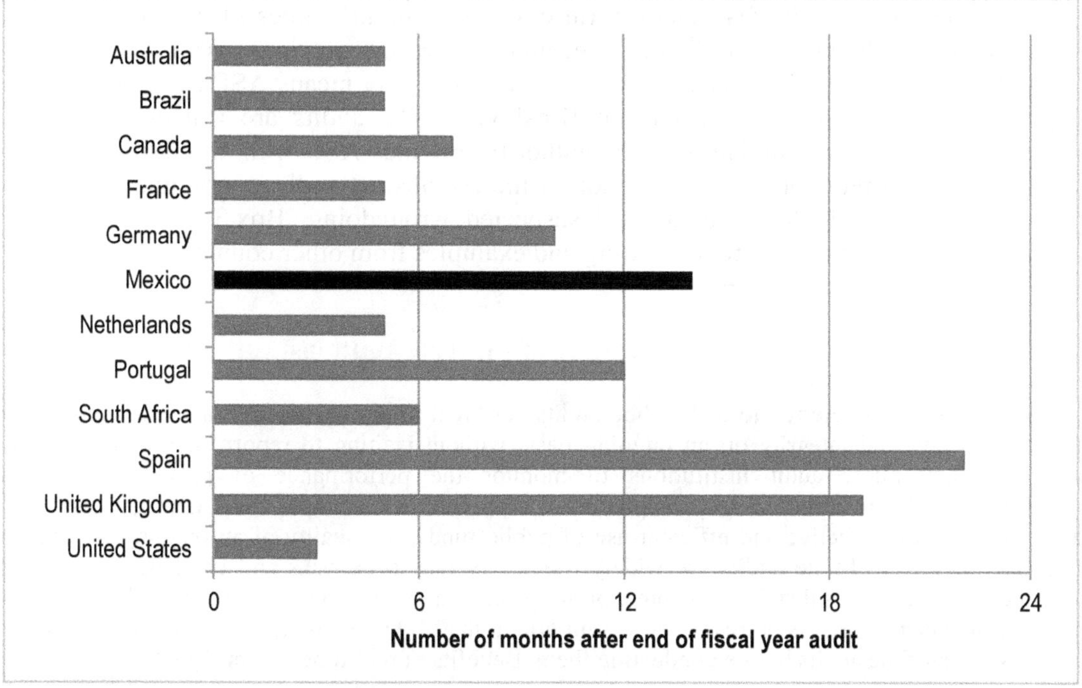

Source: OECD (2013a), *Brazil's Supreme Audit Institution: The Audit of the Consolidated Year-end Government Report*, OECD Public Governance Reviews, OECD Publishing, Paris, http://dx.doi.org/10.1787/9789264188112-en, p. 31.

Recent constitutional reforms will divide the year-end report into three reports, two of which ASF will submit to Congress at the end of June and October. These two intermediate reports are meant to divide the current year-end report into three instalments, including a third report that ASF will continue to submit 14 months following the end of the audited fiscal year, in February. The reform is intended to improve the timeliness of the information ASF provides to the legislature, so that the results of audits can assist Congress in making decisions about legislative initiatives and the budget (*Lineamientos Generales*).

The additional reporting, backed by a legislative framework, is an essential step for improving the impact of ASF's audit work for Congress. More frequent reporting also helps to further align ASF with international standards, which call for audit reports to be available promptly in order to maximise utility for consumers of the report, particularly those who must take actions in response to findings (INTOSAI, 2013a). In addition to the requirement to provide three individual audit reports, the constitutional reform grants ASF the following new authorities:

- **Early audit planning and implementation**: The recent constitutional reform allows ASF to start its audit planning and implementation earlier. First, the reform stipulates that ASF can begin auditing the month following the end of the fiscal year to be audited (i.e. in January). Prior to the reform, ASF could begin the audit process only after receiving the public account, which occurred no later than 30 April (four months after the end of the fiscal year to be audited). Second, the reform gives ASF the authority to request information from auditees during the fiscal year, in order to aid in planning and scheduling the audits it will undertake.

For instance, ASF will be able to collect information from auditees in 2017 for audits it will carry out in 2018.

- **Real-time audit authority**: The reform eliminates the principles of posteriority and annuity, allowing ASF to audit accounts before the previous fiscal year as well as audit in real time. The "real-time" audit authority means ASF can review the budget execution of the current fiscal year. The audits are triggered by "denunciations" or complaints.[2] This authority provides ASF with an additional mechanism to reorient its work outside of the established audit programme, and react quickly to high-risk areas and suspected wrongdoing. Box 3.5 provides further discussion on real-time auditing and examples from other countries.

Box 3.5. **Benefits of real-time auditing of supreme audit institutions**

Real-time audits, sometimes referred to as "ad hoc audits" or "real-time evaluations," are mechanisms for strengthening accountability and integrity on an ongoing basis without waiting to report on issues at legally mandated intervals. They allow audit institutions to monitor the performance of projects and offer recommendations to audited entities before the completion of a project. For example, an SAI might conduct a real-time audit to measure the effective and efficient use of public funds, the quality of an ongoing service, or potential wrongdoing. While real-time audits are widely used, they may pose risks and challenges that SAIs should take into account. One risk is that SAIs become, or are perceived to be, "co-decision makers", potentially compromising their independence. As a result, it is important that SAIs familiarise themselves with the drawbacks and risks of real-time audits before conducting them. Benefits of real-time audits include:

- supply in-depth, timely information to support Congress' control over the budget allocation
- aid the Executive Branch in immediately applying lessons learned from previous audit findings
- lessen risks of poor decision making and mismanagement
- allow for immediate corrective actions in response to identified irregularities outside of the normal audit programming.

INTOSAI covers real-time audits in its Peer Review Check List Guide for Supreme Audit Institutions: "Are there any rules authorising the SAI to perform audit work at an early stage of a project or programme?" (INTOSAI, 2011). SAIs worldwide employ real-time audits. For example, under the auspices of the European Neighbourhood Policy, the SAIs of Germany and Poland – the German Bundesrechnungshof (BRH) and Polish Najwyższa Izba Kontroli (NIK) - performed a twinning project at the State Audit Office of Georgia from 2014 to 2016. The project aimed at transferring knowledge and leading practices on different kinds of audit procedures, including real-time audits. In both Germany and Poland, real-time audits are performed in major projects covering infrastructure investments, defence procurement, information technology, education and market stimulation programmes. In 2010, for instance, the NIK conducted around 60 real-time audits, which included activities of public administration related to the construction sector and childcare centres, among others. The audits uncovered issues related to compliance with procurement, safety and hygiene regulations, as well as measurement of poisonous contents in nutrition.

Source: BRH (1997), "Audit Rules of the Bundesrechnungshof (Germany's Supreme Audit Institution)", www.bundesrechnungshof.de/en/bundesrechnungshof/rechtsgrundlagen/Audit%20Rules (accessed 29 February 2016); EUROSAI (2015), *Eurosai Innovations Report*, Vol. 3, Madrid, www.eurosai.org/handle404?exporturi=/export/sites/eurosai/.content/documents/strategic-plan/goal-team-1/10692-001-Eurosai-Innovations-volume-III_final-web-version.pdf (accessed 29 February 2016); NIK (2011), "Ad hoc audits at the request of the Polish Najwyższa Izba Kontroli", www.nik.gov.pl/en/news/ad-hoc-audits-at-the-request-of-the-nik.html (accessed 29 February 2016); State Audit Office of Georgia (SAO) (2015), *Twinning SAO-BRH-NIK Newsletter*, Vol. 1, Tbilisi, http://sao.ge/files/auditi/publications/01_Quarterly%20Newsletter_EN.pdf (accessed 29 February 2016).

ASF has yet to determine how it will strategically use these new authorities, such as how it will integrate early audit planning or real-time audits into its traditional audit programming and implementation, if at all. A major consideration in this regard is alignment with the "Annual Programme of Audits for the Public Account" (PAAF) and ASF's risk-based audit programming. Currently, ASF approves the PAAF in May, and then plans and implements thousands of audits through the following January. For instance, ASF approved the PAAF for the public account of 2013 and sent it to ASF's Vigilance Committee (Comisión de Vigilancia de la Auditoria Superior de la Federación, or CVASF) on 30 May 2014. The PAAF consisted of nearly 1 200 audits and 16 studies on various themes (ASF, *Informes de Actividades*).

The timeline of the PAAF and the large volume of audits it covers raises a number of strategic considerations, including the following:

- ASF could consider how it will effectively align early audit planning and implementation with its PAAF, since it can start planning for audits in the previous fiscal year and begin conducting audits in January, five months before completing its audit programming.
- ASF could consider how real-time audits will be used to complement and add value to existing audit programming, if at all, given the already high volume of audits that make up the PAAF.
- Similarly, ASF could consider using real-time audits as inputs to its own risk assessments. For instance, prevalence of a high volume of complaints in a specific sector or ministry could inform the analysis and scoring of the likelihood and impact of risks during audit programming.

ASF officials commented that they are unlikely to incorporate real-time audits into traditional audit programming, since they are triggered by complaints. Nonetheless, a high volume of real-time audits resulting from complaints could divert resources away from traditional audit programming, which reflects strategic priorities and high risks. If such audits are not incorporated into programming, at a minimum they can be used as inputs. This is akin to using investigations to inform audits of systemic internal control deficiencies, recognising that the strengths of ASF is primarily in its preventive, birds-eye view of issues in government. The following section further elaborates on considerations for ASF in developing a plan to use its new audit authorities strategically and in line with its current audit programming.

ASF could focus its audits early in the fiscal year on high-risk programmes, as well as programme performance, in order to increase the value of reports for the budgetary decision-making process.

Supreme audit institutions should publish reports that are timely and relevant for the budgetary cycle (OECD, 2015). Recent reforms, as described above, are a positive step toward improving the timeliness of ASF's reports. However, producing more reports on its own does not equate to timeliness or utility value for decision makers. A comparison between the cycles for audit reporting and the budgetary process helps to illustrate why.

As shown in Figure 3.2, Congress will have limited time to consider both of ASF's additional reports to make budgetary decisions. ASF will need to deliver its first report to the Chamber of Deputies by 30 June. This report is timely in that it provides Congress at least four months to consider the information before passing the Revenue Act in October and approving the budget in November of the same fiscal year. However, ASF's second audit report, delivered by 31 October, is less timely for informing budgetary decision making. Specifically, the report may not be available to inform the passing of the Revenue Act, which occurs on the same date of the delivery of the audit report. Moreover, Congress would effectively have two weeks to consider the report ahead of the budget approval on 15 November. ASF has yet to decide how it will divide the three reports, but given the scope of ASF's year-end audit, this does not appear to be sufficient time for effective use of the October report for the budget cycle.[3]

Figure 3.2. **Comparison of audit reporting and budget cycles in Mexico illustrates time constraints for Congress to use ASF's reports**

Audit reporting cycle for previous fiscal year (fiscal year X-1)	Fiscal Year X	Budget forumulation cycle for next fiscal year (fiscal year X+1)
1st - Following the constitutional reform, ASF may start auditing activites for the previous fiscal year	January	
30th - The Ministry of Economy sends the public account for previous fiscal year to the Chamber of Deputies	April	**1st** - The Executive sends Congress revenues and expenditures' objectives, projections and priorities for the next fiscal year
2nd - The Vigilance Committee (CVASF) of the Chamber of Deputies receives the account of previous fiscal year **4th** - After intial review, the CVASF forwards the account of the previous year to the ASF and to the Committee on Budgets and Public Accounts (CBPA) of the Chamber of Deputies	May	
30th - ASF delivers first audit report to the Chamber of Deputies on account of previous fiscal year	June	**30th** - The Executive sends to Chamber of Deputies a progress report on programmes approved for current budget, as well as details and justification for new proposals (expenditures only)
	September	**8th** - Executive submits draft budget of revenues and expenditures for next fiscal year
31th - ASF delivers second audit report to the Chamber of Deputies on account of previous fiscal year	October	**31st** - Revenue Act passed by both Chambers of the Congress
	November	**15th** - The Chamber of Deputies approves expenditure budget
	Fiscal Year X+1	
20th - ASF submits the third audit report as well as the report on the results of audits to the Chamber of Deputies	February	
30th - The CVASF submits observations and recommendations as well as analysis of the ASF Report to the CBPA	May	
31st - The Chamber of Deputies approves the public account and terminates the audit cycle (30th of September according to the Federal Auditing Law)	October	

The audit report that ASF will be required to submit each June offers the best opportunity to enhance the relevance of its work as an input for the budgeting process. Therefore, when determining its audit priorities early in the year, ASF could consider how it can maximise the utility of the June report for the Congress and its budget deliberations. Legislatures and their committees require an adequate amount of time to reflect upon and debate budget documentation prior to approval. This is particularly important in order to ensure that legislative committees have sufficient time to review, debate, and propose amendments (OECD, 2011). This could include prioritisation of high-risk areas for audits conducted early in the fiscal year, as well as performance audits that focus on financial and operational performance. Tailoring the reports will reflect the possibility that the three individual reports may serve different purposes as inputs for Congress, based on the budgetary cycle as well as legislative initiatives.

Strengthening accountability by improving the uptake of ASF's audits

Congress could build its own technical capacity in order to increase uptake of inputs from ASF and the SNF.

Congress should scrutinise audit reports the SAI prepares in a timely manner (OECD, 2002). Public Accounts Committees (PACs) are often responsible for this role, as is the case in Mexico. Moreover, as a part of its oversight functions, Congress examines the execution of the state budget and it is common in OECD countries for the legislature to either formally (as in the case of a discharge procedure) or informally (implicitly) give a political opinion on the way the executive has executed the budget (OECD, 2002 and 2014a). Studies on the oversight role of the Legislature and PACs highlight numerous barriers to effectively providing such oversight. For instance, legislators may fail to take oversight of government accounts seriously because doing so has little benefit for re-election or it could risk backlash from one's party (Hoque, 2015). The implication is that the presence of PACs on its own does not necessarily equate to effective oversight.

In addition to ASF, the two key entities responsible for accountability and oversight in Mexico at the federal level are the Vigilance Committee (CVASF) and the Committee on Budget and Public Accounts (Comisión de Presupuesto y Cuenta Pública, or CPCP). Among other duties, the Vigilance Committee is responsible for co-ordinating relations between the Chamber of Deputies and ASF. The Chamber of Deputies, according to Article 74 of the Mexican Constitution, is responsible for approving the public budget. ASF is accountable to the Chamber of Deputies, and in particular, to its Vigilance Committee and its Evaluation and Control Unit (Unidad de Evaluación y Control, or UEC). The UEC is in charge of monitoring the performance of ASF and its officials.

As indicated above, a key step in the process for approving the public account is the CVASF's analysis of ASF's audit report, before it sends its own report to the CPCP with conclusions and recommendations. For instance, in May 2015, CVASF submitted a reported to CPCP with analysis, findings, and recommendations related to over 1 400 audits conducted by ASF for the 2013 public account. CVASF considers numerous sources to inform its analysis and develop its report, including the UEC's analyses of ASF's year-end report and results of meetings between the CVASF and other Congressional committees. Moreover, the CVASF asks all other committees to submit opinions in writing regarding ASF's report.

Such consultative approaches are, in theory, practical ways to involve a wide range of Congressional stakeholders in the accountability process and solicit diverse perspectives. In practice, however, opportunities remain for Congress to contribute more to oversight and the audit cycle, in accordance with their statutory obligations. For instance, Figure 3.3 shows a reduction in the percentage of Congressional committees that provide opinions on ASF's year-end report, particularly since 2011 (ASF, 2015b). The percentages for 2009 and 2010 in Figure 3.3 are based on a total of 43 committees, and for the remaining years, there were 55 committees in the Chamber of Deputies. For instance, in 2013, only 4 of 55 committees in the Chamber of Deputies provided CVASF with an opinion on the accounts.

Figure 3.3. **The percentage of Congressional committees that issued opinions on ASF's public accounts report less than one-third**

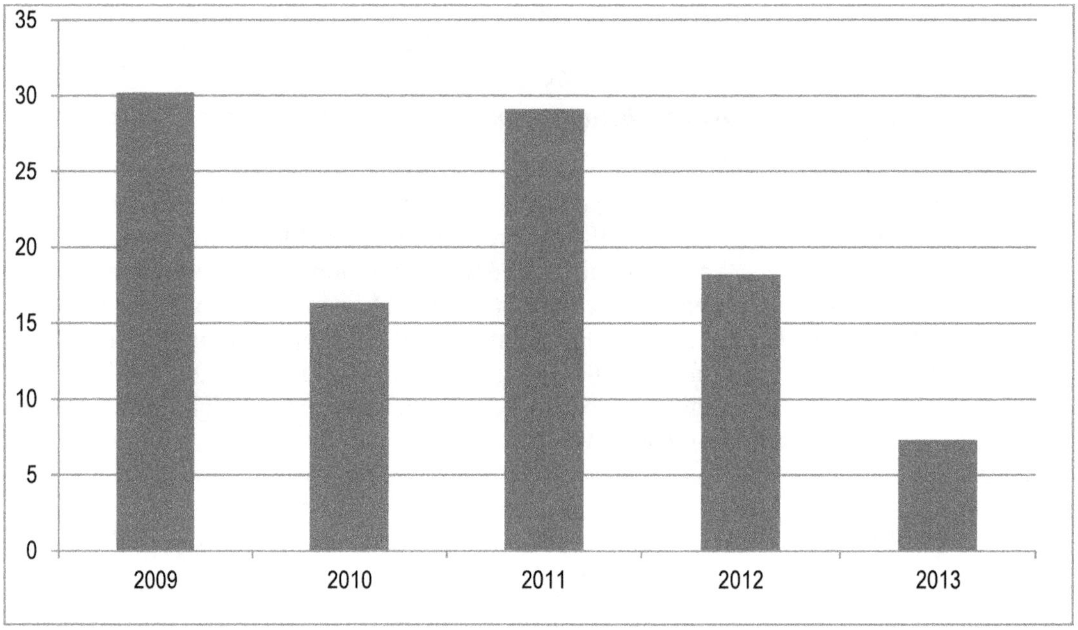

Source: Adapted from: ASF (2015b), "Panorama de la fiscalización en México", ASF Publishing, Mexico City, www3.diputados.gob.mx/camara/content/download/334211/1191134/file/Libro%20Panorama%20de%20la%20Fiscalizacion%20Superior%202015.pdf.

In addition, while the full house of the Chamber of Deputies has statutory responsibilities to approve the budget, it has failed to do so on a consistent basis. Specifically, as illustrated in Figure 3.4, the process of analysing and formulating an opinion on the public account is still in progress for 8 out of the 14 years since 2000 (Congress of Mexico, 2015). For those eight years, the accountability and audit cycle, as envisioned in the Mexican Constitution and legislation, is incomplete.

Figure 3.4. **Congressional opinion of the public account is incomplete for 8 of the 14 years from 2000 to 2013**

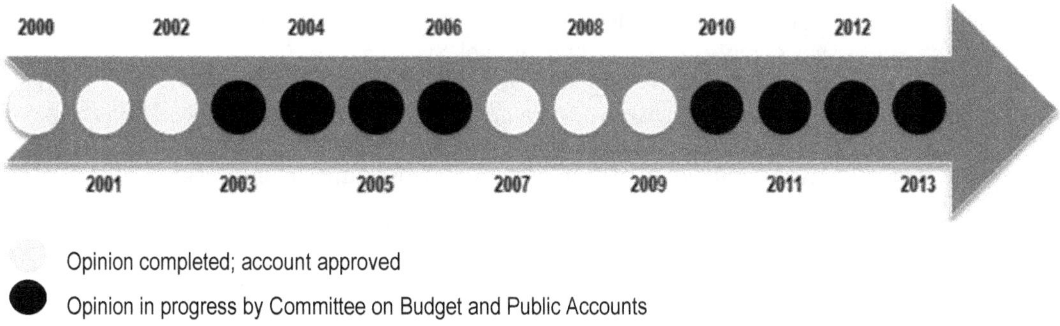

Source: Adapted from Congress of Mexico (2015), "Nota Informa sobre la normativa concerniente al dictamen de la cuenta de la hacienda pública federal", 29 September.

Other factors, besides political economy and political will, are also likely to influence the level of Congress's engagement in the auditing cycle. In particular, the need to develop the technical capacity to support committees was highlighted in OECD interviews. Certain committees lack technical support altogether, and some committees with support (i.e. "assessors") are financed by political parties and work for specific deputies within the Chamber, as opposed to the committee itself. Having a stronger technical capacity among committees would increase the knowledge and expertise to actually use ASF's reports effectively to improve legislative initiatives, budget processes, and other issues of concern for committees. According to representatives of the CVASF, committees need subject matter experts to help them interpret the information in ASF's reports, but this function is not institutionalised in the Chambers. Investing and building this capacity within Congress is a critical step for improving policy making, and the accountability process as a whole, in Mexico.

ASF could assess its internal quality-control processes in order to ensure the relevance and quality of its products for Congress amid additional reporting requirements.

Reports that are not accessible or readable for a broader audience, or scoped inappropriately for key users, can undermine the very purpose of compiling the report in the first place. INTOSAI's Fundamental Principles of Public-Sector Auditing notes "reports should be easy to understand, free from vagueness or ambiguity and complete. They should be objective and fair, only including information which is supported by sufficient and appropriate audit evidence and ensuring that findings are put into perspective and context" (INTOSAI, 2013a). Moreover, INTOSAI's Quality Control for SAIs states that SAIs should ensure that their risk-management procedures, which can include carefully scoping the work to be performed, are adequate to mitigate risks of carrying out the work (INTOSAI, 2010a). As demonstrated by the example from the Netherlands in Box 3.6, the quality of audit reports is a function of not only the readability and clarity of the report, but also the quality assurance processes applied to the design and implementation of the audit itself.

Box 3.6. The Netherlands Court of Audits and its three quality control points

The Netherlands Court of Audits (NCA) uses an internal quality control system to conduct high-quality audits that comply with the International Standards of Supreme Audit Institutions (ISSAI). The system includes "three control points" that occurs during the design, implementation, and completion phases of the audit. As detailed below, the final control point focuses on improving the quality and readability of the audit to help ensure that the findings are communicated effectively and will have an impact. NCA's three control points include the following:

1. The Court's Performance Audit Information Centre acts as a source of advance information for auditors. It assesses the definition of the audit problem and the audit questions, and advises auditors on how to perform the audit with maximum effectiveness and efficiency.
2. During the course of an audit, a team of fellow auditors advises on the technical and strategic quality of the audit. Specifically, these teams issue advisory reports to the directors of the Court's audit department during the course of audits.
3. Once an audit has been completed, the Quality Assurance and Control Division performs a quality assurance assessment. This involves assessing the clarity and readability of the draft audit report, as well as the validity, reliability, consistency and added value of the audit. Based on its findings, the Division makes suggestions to the Board for improvement in the audit.

Source: The Netherlands Court of Audits (2012), "Quality control", *2011 Annual Report Online*, www.courtofaudit.nl/english/2011_Annual_report/2011_Annual_report:17798/Audits/Quality_control.

In recent years, the quality of ASF's reporting appears to have adhered to international best practices and standards for quality assurance. For instance, a peer review of ASF in 2009 by three supreme audit institutions found that the quality assurance system of ASF's Performance Audit Office (Auditoría Especial de Desempeño) had processes for monitoring the quality of audit work and goes beyond international standards (Puerto Rico Office of the Comptroller, UK National Audit Office and US Government Accountability, 2008). Moreover, in 2009, ASF strengthened its quality control and assurance system by further aligning its practices with international standards and best practices, which included a recertification of its processes according to the International Organization of Standardization (ISO 9001:2000).

In an unpublished OECD survey of supreme audit institutions in 2013, conducting surveys were one of the most common techniques that respondent SAIs used to ensure relevant, adequate and effective quality control (OECD, 2013b). Surveys can focus on internal aspects of SAIs operations to ensure quality control, or they can be client surveys, which aim to obtain perspectives from key users of the SAI's work, including legislators and audited entities. ASF hired a prominent university in Mexico, the Centre for Research and Teachings in Economics (Centro de Investigación y Docencia Económicas, or CIDE), who conducted a study of ASF called, "Knowledge, Utility and Areas of Improvement for Supreme Audit", in order understand the perception of different users of ASF's work. Box 3.7 provides examples of SAIs that use client surveys to enhance the quality of their work.

Box 3.7. Supreme audit institutions that survey key users to assess quality of audit work

Australia

After each performance audit report is complete, the Australian National Audit Office (ANAO) seeks feedback on the audit process by means of a survey and an interview with the responsible manager of the audited entity. The survey is an important tool for improving the quality and effectiveness of performance audit services. Survey results provide an insight into the effectiveness of current practice and inform the development of new audit practices and approaches. The survey is designed by a firm of consultants that is engaged by the ANAO but independent of the performance audit teams. The response rate from auditees surveyed for the 2011–12 reporting period was 75% and 87% in 2010-11.

Key matters on which feedback is sought include the audit process; audit reporting; and the value of the ANAO's performance audit services more generally. For instance, in the 2011-12 survey, the proportion of respondents that acknowledged the value added by ANAO services was 91% (up from 86% in 2010–11). The percentage of respondents that considered the auditors had demonstrated the professional knowledge and audit skills required to conduct the audit was 85% (down from 91% in 2010–11).

Denmark

Rigsrevisionen, the SAI of Denmark, has used a variety of techniques to assess its benefits to audited entities and to the governance system, including client surveys. For instance, in 2009, Rigsrevisionen hired a consultancy firm to conduct an independent client survey on their behalf. The clients included permanent secretaries, director generals, managing directors of government-owned companies, financial managers, other officials in central government and members of the Parliament's Public Accounts Committee.

Rigsrevisionen officials were most interested in understanding how their clients experienced the quality of services offered, their working relationship and the usefulness of their audit findings. The survey identified areas for improvement across four areas: financial auditing (annual audit); performance auditing (major examinations); co-ordination, planning and counselling; and interaction with the Public Accounts Committee. The findings included recommendations to become more responsive during the audit phase in which memoranda and draft reports are being prepared, and to raise the competencies of SAI staff to a more uniform level.

New Zealand

The New Zealand Office of the Auditor General (OAG) uses an independent firm to conduct an annual client satisfaction survey of public entities audited by the Auditor General. The firm surveys a random sample of public entities to measure the level of satisfaction and identify areas where OAG needs to improve their audit services. Before 2007/08, the survey sample was confined to public entities audited by OAG. In 2007/08, OAG extended the sample to cover public entities audited by private sector accounting firms. Representatives of a sample of these entities are invited to participate in a telephone interview to provide comment and to rate the following factors on a scale from 1 to 10, with 1 being very low and 10 being very high:

- audit service providers' core audit ability
- audit service providers' staff knowledge
- the way audit service providers' staff work with entities, including governing bodies and audit committees where relevant
- the value that audit service providers add and the usefulness of the advice given
- the performance and contribution that audit service providers made as entities prepared to adopt New Zealand Equivalents to International Financial Reporting Standards (NZ IFRS)
- the overall degree of satisfaction with the service received from audit service provider.

The results of client surveys are prominently displayed in OAG's annual reports, including in the preface by the Auditor General. Doing so communicates the importance of the surveys to OAG staff, as well as alertness among the leadership of the importance of meeting stakeholders' and clients' evolving needs.

Source: OECD (2014b), *Chile's Supreme Audit Institution: Enhancing Strategic Agility and Public Trust*, OECD Public Governance Reviews, OECD Publishing, Paris, http://dx.doi.org/10.1787/9789264207561-en; New Zealand Controller and Auditor-General (2009), "Annual Report 2008-2009", Office of the Auditor-General, New Zealand, www.oag.govt.nz/2009/2008-09/docs/annual-report.pdf.

While there are positive examples that exemplify ASF's attention to quality, the expanded reporting requirements of ASF will place new demands on its internal policies and processes for maintaining relevance and quality. In addition, in interviews with OECD, some users of ASF's work, including Congress and civil society organisations, voiced concerns about the usefulness of ASF's reports. For instance, interviewees said the audit reports overuse technical language, or are organised in a way that makes it difficult to analyse them. Moreover, a representative of a Congressional committee said ASF's audits sometimes have too narrow a scope, in that they focus on a sub-programme or project, which undermines the usefulness of the report for analysing the performance of broader programmes. This feedback from key users of ASF's work suggests the need for further evaluation about the root causes of such issues, particularly in light of additional reporting requirements that will be required of ASF.

To address potential concerns about the utility value of its work, ASF could assess its current processes and procedures for maintaining quality control, and anticipate potential risks to quality that might arise in order to meet new reporting demands. In addition to peer reviews, where appropriate, ASF can consider other means of monitoring the quality of its work beyond surveys or feedback from clients like Congressional committees, auditees, and civil society organisations, or procedures for receiving and dealing with complaints about the quality of its work, per international standards (INTOSAI, 2010a). For instance, ASF could identify potential changes to its audit programming- the Annual Programme of Audits for the Public Account (Programa Anual de Auditorías para la Fiscalización Superior de la Cuenta Pública, or PAAF) – in order to enhance the relevance of its work for the Congress. The programming model of ASF is based on an analysis of 16 risk factors, which are weighed and used in selecting audits. One of these 16 variables involves requests from Congress. When ASF receives a petition from Congress, it allocates a level of risk for the specific subject in the request. The risk scoring reflects the relevance of the potential irregularities related in the request. However, additional changes to audit programming could help ASF to further align the scope of its audits with the needs and interests of its users, particularly Congress.

One approach ASF could consider is to adapt its proposal form (shown in Figure 3.5) to require teams to indicate the Congressional committees they believe would be interested in the results of the audits. As discussed in Chapter 1, the process of audit programming involves individual audit units, which present proposals for specific audits. This additional information could be included in the justification section of the form that teams submit for audit proposals (see "justificación" in Figure 3.5). This would encourage teams to consider a potential user of the audit results, and the scope of information relevant to inform legislative initiatives or budget decisions. This justification could be used to help facilitate the discussion and selection phase during audit programming. Moreover, ASF could then compile this information to inform Congress of its plans for audits that are relevant to the themes and challenges facing individual committees (see next section on the communication strategy with Congress).

Figure 3.5. **ASF's form for submitting audit proposals**

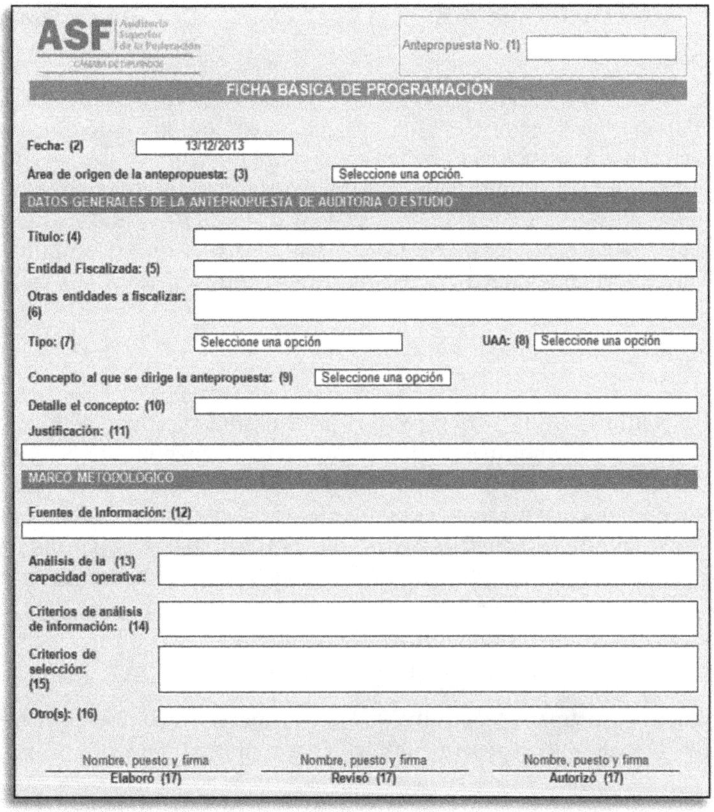

ASF Auditoría Superior de la Federación
CÁMARA DE DIPUTADOS

Anteproupesta No. (1)

FICHA BÁSICA DE PROGRAMACIÓN

Fecha: (2) 13/12/2013

Área de origen de la anteproupesta: (3) Seleccione una opción.

DATOS GENERALES DE LA ANTEPROPUESTA DE AUDITORÍA O ESTUDIO

Título: (4)

Entidad Fiscalizada: (5)

Otras entidades a fiscalizar: (6)

Tipo: (7) Seleccione una opción

UAA: (8) Seleccione una opción

Concepto al que se dirige la anteproupesta: (9) Seleccione una opción

Detalle el concepto: (10)

Justificación: (11)

MARCO METODOLÓGICO

Fuentes de Información: (12)

Análisis de la (13) capacidad operativa:

Criterios de análisis de información: (14)

Criterios de selección: (15)

Otro(s): (16)

Nombre, puesto y firma	Nombre, puesto y firma	Nombre, puesto y firma
Elaboró (17)	Revisó (17)	Autorizó (17)

Source: ASF (2015c), "Planning and Programming of the Audit of the Public Account of ASF" [Planeación y Programación para la Fiscalización de la Cuenta Pública en la ASF], ASF presentation at the OECD fact-finding mission, October 2015.

ASF and state audit institutions could enhance outreach, communication strategies and trainings to improve the relevance and impact of their work among key stakeholders, including Congress, its committees, auditees and citizens.

A more strategic approach for engaging Congress, particularly in light of additional reporting requirements throughout the year, could help to enhance ASF's impact and relevance for this key user of its work. ASF's annual reporting to Congress and the general public is in line with the INTOSAI's "Lima Declaration of Guidelines on Auditing Precepts" (INTOSAI, 1977: § 16). However, challenges remain with regard to communicating the added value of ASF to Congress and its committees. According to SNF members, there appears to be a misconception and lack of understanding in Congress about the purpose and benefits of ASF. One factor that is likely to influence this is the high level of turnover within Congress, which in turn places an additional burden on ASF to routinely explain its added value. Moreover, much of the current communication between ASF and Congress is ad hoc. An effective communication strategy could help ASF to communicate not only its value, but that of the SNF, to Congress. Box 3.8 provides examples of SAIs' outreach to Congress.

Box 3.8. Supreme audit institutions' experiences with congressional outreach

Sweden

Every four years following the general election, new members are appointed to the Swedish Parliamentary Committees. To ensure that these new members better understand the work of the Swedish National Audit Office (SNAO) once the Committees are constituted, the SNAO invites representatives to visit the office. During these visits, the Auditors General and staff: 1) provide an overview of the SNAO and its mission; and 2) describe the ongoing audit activities and planned audits that may fall within the visiting Committee's area of interest. The meeting format is relatively informal and encourages questions and discussions. As such, it is an opportunity for knowledge exchange and networking.

United Kingdom

The work of the UK National Audit office (NAO) informs the scrutiny of government by parliamentary select committees, particularly the Committee of Public Accounts, for whom the NAO provides a wide range of reports, briefings and other analysis to support their hearings into the value for money of public spending. The NAO also supports other parliamentary select committees on issues where it has expertise relevant to their inquiries. To inform these committees about its work, the NAO prepares departmental overview reports that summarise its work on each major department, and shares these with the relevant parliamentary select committees in advance of the annual reviews of government departments that they carry out. Departmental overviews provide an array of useful information for the committees about the NAO's work that is about the Executive department relevant to the committees' area of interest, including:

- a summary of their department's activity and performance over the past year, based primarily on published sources, including the department's own accounts and the work of the NAO
- information on how the department is organised, where it spends its money, recent and planned changes to the department's spending and any major changes or developments in policies and how they were delivered
- major developments that the department has planned for the coming year, such as major structural changes, new policies that will come into force, legislation that is going through Parliament, and any large contracts that have to be renegotiated
- main findings of its most recent financial audit of the department's accounts that would be of interest to the committee
- a summary of key findings of any value for money, performance improvement or investigative work it carries out on the department over the last year and what the department has committed to do in response.

Source: EUROSAI (2014), "Sharing good practices among Supreme Audit Institutions", *EUROSAI Innovations: Volume II*, www.eurosai.org/handle404?exporturi=/export/sites/eurosai/.content/documents/strategic-plan/goal-team-1/Innovations-volume-II_Web.pdf.

In addition, as discussed, steps could be taken to develop a more constructive working relationship with auditees, which can ultimately lead to improved absorption of audit recommendations. While this relationship depends in part on the quality of ASF's work and relevance of the recommendations made, a communication strategy for interacting with auditees that articulates shared goals and improvements to governance would help to align ASF with best practices and international standards. For instance, ISSAI and INTOSAI guidelines establish a number of leading practices for SAIs to engage with auditees and responsible parties. Box 3.9 provides additional information on relevant standards.

Box 3.9. Selected standards for supreme audit institutions' communication with auditees

INTOSAI's "Fundamental Principles of Public Sector Auditing" (INTOSAI, 2013a) recognise that SAIs should enhance good communications with auditees in order to develop a constructive working relationship. This communication may include information on the responsibilities of the auditor and auditee throughout the audit cycle and the objective, scope and timing of audit engagements. Moreover, these principles state that SAIs should ensure that the terms of audit engagements have been clearly established in writing, communicated and understood by the auditee and responsible parties (INTOSAI, 2013a: § 48). INTOSAI's guidance on "How to Increase the Use and Impact of Audit Reports" notes that the relationship between the SAI and the auditee can be greatly improved if the SAI sets up communication protocols (INTOSAI, 2010b). Finally, INTOSAI's "Principles of Transparency and Accountability" note that SAIs should consider adopting objective and transparent audit standards, processes and methods (INTOSAI, 2010c).

Source: INTOSAI (2013a), "Fundamental Principles of Compliance Auditing", INTOSAI Professional Standards Committee, Copenhagen, www.issai.org/media/69912/issai-400-english.pdf; INTOSAI (2010b), "Principles for Transparency and Accountability", INTOSAI Professional Standards Committee, Copenhagen, www.issai.org/media/12930/issai_20_e_.pdf; INTOSAI (2010c), "Internal Audit Independence in the Public Sector", www.issai.org/media/13349/intosai_gov_9140_e_.pdf.

Other key audiences for ASF's work include civil society organisations (CSOs), media, research organisations, private entities, and the public in general. Such actors are on the "demand side of governance," and play important roles in promoting effective governance, transparency and accountability. They are also potential users of ASF that analyse, disseminate, and act on its information and reports. SAIs demonstrate ongoing relevance to citizens and other stakeholders, in part, through effective communication (Effective Institutions Platform, 2014). ASF has an office dedicated to monitoring and co-ordinating communication strategies. This office will play a critical role to address many of ASF's challenges for communicating its work and substantiating its relevance to key external stakeholders.

In light of ongoing challenges ASF faces to communicate its value and results to an array of stakeholders, ASF could consider developing an outreach and communication strategy to clarify how ASF intends its users to take advantage of its work. Such a strategy would complement ASF's existing efforts, including its informal discussions with Congress, and it could aid in the following:

- Defining core target audiences, and in the process, discern their understanding of the work of both ASF and SNF. More precision in terms of how ASF defines its audiences can be of greater value for a strategy than general categories. For instance, instead of identifying the Congress as a key audience, ASF could consider specific committees that reflect core users. Moreover, audiences can be grouped into tiers based on their level of importance (e.g. primary, secondary, etc.).
- Having defined target audiences, a strategy should have clear and measurable communication objectives for each target audience.

- Communication strategies can adopt different approaches and mechanisms for achieving the defined objectives (see Box 3.10). The strategy should clearly define roles and allocated resources.
- Evaluation, monitoring, and a feedback loop are critical elements of a communication strategy, which allow for incorporating lessons learned from communication activities.

In line with efforts to improve outreach and communication, ASF could also consider using executive summaries, one-page "highlights," or "snapshots" to present main findings and recommendations from specific audits. These products are derivative of full reports, and therefore require few resources and time to compile. Moreover, they could help ASF to target its communication to specific audiences, such as select Congressional committees that may have an interest in a specific programme or policy. To help auditors and staff to use such tools and improve their ability to formulate messages, ASF could consider refining its existing trainings on report writing to include a focus on messaging and communicating concise findings.

Box 3.10. Communication strategy at the supreme audit institution of Costa Rica

In the 1990s, the Controller General of the Republic (Contraloria General de la Republica, or CGR) established a Press and Communication Unit (Unidad de Prensa y Comunicaciones, or UPC) aimed at establishing formal linkages with the media in order to disseminate the results of audit activities. After establishing this unit, the CGR began to inform *ex-officio* about audit reports, resolutions, and studies, as well as to disseminate other documents related to its oversight activities that were considered to be of public interest. In 2006, the CGR understood that it also needed to reach out to Congress, diverse sectors of Costa Rican society, as well as to the general public, and decided to bolster its existing strategy.

The existence of a formal organic structure to support this policy, as well as its acknowledgement in CGR's strategic plan, are indicators of the high level of institutionalisation underpinning the policy. Specifically, the UPC took the lead in implementing a broader communication strategy, which was consolidated in 2008 through the approval of the 2008-12 Strategic Plan. The plan acknowledged citizens as major actors in the oversight process, and included among its objectives: increasing the use of audit products by Congress, the media, and the general public (Objective 5), and improving citizens' trust in the CGR. The information and communication policy became a high-priority strategic objective for the CGR, expanding the universe of actors that receive information about CGR's activities and relying on innovative channels to communicate with the public (including for example, a citizen newsletter, press releases, and a YouTube channel, among others).

Source: Guillan Montero, Aranzazu (2012), "Building bridges: Advancing transparency and participation through the articulation of supreme audit institutions and civil society", paper presented at the 2nd Transatlantic Conference on Transparency Research, Utrecht, 7-9 June (as cited in Effective Institutions Platform, 2014).

State audit institutions (Entidades de Fiscalización Superior Estatales, or EFSEs) could apply the same lessons as ASF to improve understanding of its work among stakeholders and improve citizen participation through targeted communication strategies. Greater understanding of EFSEs' audits and reports can help to strengthen accountability and integrity. For instance, the Superior Audit Institution of Puebla (Auditoría Superior del Estado de Puebla, or ASEP) established several co-operation agreements with educational institutions, as well as with Puebla's Ministry of Education, to educate the citizenry on ethical values and develop a culture of accountability in the use of public resources. ASEP's website also has a section on "Audit for children" to help promote greater awareness about its work and role in government.[4]

Outreach and a strategy for engagement with stakeholders can also facilitate whistleblowing and referral mechanisms. For example, ASEP has established an "Ethics Hotline" for citizens to file complaints, information regarding potential fraud or crimes in the use of public resources, and corruption-related incidents. Moreover, if important information and key documents are published by default, citizens, academics, the press, public opinion leaders and social organisations will be able to analyse them and hold state legislatures accountable for the follow-up of audit results. This formula of publicity and citizen engagement would provide additional safeguards to EFSEs to carry out their work with objectivity and impartiality.

Proposals for action

ASF, like all SAIs, operates from a unique vantage point in government that allows them to look across institutions during their reviews to identify issues of systemic importance and strengthen coherence. **ASF could apply its comparative advantage in auditing to lead government-wide studies and audits of the implementation of the National Transparency System's strategy to strengthen transparency.** In addition, although ASF has the power to conduct investigations and forensic audits, its expertise and knowledge of cross-cutting issues in government related to internal control systems can be better leveraged. **ASF could conduct, to complement its forensic audits and investigations, evaluations of systemic deficiencies in internal control and risk management to improve broader governance functions.**

To make effective use of its new authorities, it is critical for ASF to plan strategically and consider how it might integrate new responsibilities into existing processes and procedures. One strategic consideration involves its use of real-time audits and ability to start audits earlier in the year. **ASF could help ensure the timeliness and uptake of its work in Congress by effectively aligning its new authorities, such as early audit planning and conducting real-time audits, with its traditional audit programming.** As part of this strategic thinking, ASF can consider how to maximise its value and input to Congressional decision making. **ASF could focus its audits early in the fiscal year on high-risk programmes, as well as programme performance, in order to increase the value of reports for the budgetary decision-making process.**

Ensuring the impact and relevance of ASF's work is not just a matter of strategic considerations. In addition, Congress, as a critical actor in a system of accountability, can also take actions to ensure use of audits and findings from audit institutions. **Congress could build its own technical capacity in order to increase uptake of inputs from ASF and the SNF. Moreover, ASF could assess its internal quality-control processes in order to ensure the relevance and quality of its products for Congress amid additional reporting requirements.** Such actions are vital for ensuring the uptake of recommendations and findings, but additional steps can be taken to improve engagement with audit institutions' external stakeholders, including Congress and citizenry. **ASF and state audit institutions could enhance outreach, communication strategies and trainings to improve the relevance and impact of their work among key stakeholders, including Congress, its committees, auditees and citizens.**

Notes

1. In 2009, ASF established a forensic audit and investigative function to combat fraud and corruption identified during audits of the year-end account. The Special Financial Compliance Auditor, a division in ASF, is responsible for co-ordinating and supervising ASF's forensic audits. The Director General of Forensic Audits (DGFA), which is under this entity, leads the operational aspects of conducting forensic audits and investigations, including the review of processes, facts or evidence for detecting and investigating irregularities or unlawful conduct (ASF, 2014). DGFA does not have the legal authority to conduct covert testing, such as undercover work to identify internal control deficiencies.
2. According to the constitutional reform, there are two conditions that must be met in order for ASF to carry out real-time audits: 1) it must stem from a report (denunciation); and 2) it must be endorsed by the Auditor General of Mexico.
3. ASF's year-end report for 2014 is nearly 400 pages long and reflects over 1 600 individual audits.
4. For more information, see www.auditoriapuebla.gob.mx/auditoria-para-ninos.

References

ASF (Auditoria Superior de la Federación) (2015a), "Technical Study for the Promotion of a Culture of Integrity in the Public Sector", http://asf.gob.mx/uploads/180_Estudios/1173_Estudio_Tec_para_la_Promocion_de_la_Cultura_de_Integridad_en_el_Sec_Pub.pdf.

ASF (2015b), "Panorama de la fiscalización en México", ASF Publishing, Mexico City, www3.diputados.gob.mx/camara/content/download/334211/1191134/file/Libro%20Panorama%20de%20la%20Fiscalizacion%20Superior%202015.pdf.

ASF (2015c), "Planning and Programming of the Audit of the Public Account of ASF" [Planeación y Programación para la Fiscalización de la Cuenta Pública en la ASF], ASF presentation at the OECD fact-finding mission, October 2015.

ASF (2014), "Study about the Strategies for Combating Corruption in the Public Sector", http://informe.asf.gob.mx/Documentos/Auditorias/2014_1642_a.pdf.

ASF (2013), "Continuation to the Studies of Internal Control and the Diffusion of the Study of Integrity in the Public Sector", http://asf.gob.mx/uploads/180_Estudios/1198_Continuidad_a_los_Estudios_de_Control_Interno_y_a_la_Difusion_del_Estudio_de_Integridad_en_el_Sector_Publico.pdf.

ASF (2012), "General Study of the Conditions of the Institutional Internal Control System in the Federal Public Sector", http://asf.gob.mx/uploads/180_Estudios/1172_Estudio_General_de_la_Situacion_que_Guarda_el_Sistema_de_Control_Interno_Institucional_en_el_Sector_Publico_Federal.pdf.

ASF (2011) "Plan Estratégiade la ASF (2011-2017)", January, Mexico City, www.asf.gob.mx/uploads/58_/Plan_Estrategico_ASF_2011-2017_web.pdf.

BAI (Board of Audit and Inspection) (2013), "Audit on the status of public information sharing", 25 July, http://bai.go.kr/cmm/fdm/FileDown.do?atchFileId=2013072514002351 8&fileSn=1&siteId=bai&bbsId=BBSMSTR_100000000009

BRH (Bundesrechnungshof) (1997), "Audit Rules of the Bundesrechnungshof (Germany's Supreme Audit Institution)", www.bundesrechnungshof.de/en/bundesrechnungshof/rechtsgrundlagen/Audit%20Rules (accessed 29 February 2016).

Congress of Mexico (2015), "Nota Informa sobre la normative concerniente al dictamen de la cuenta de la hacienda publica fédéral", 29 September.

Effective Institutions Platform (2014), "Supreme Audit Institutions and Stakeholder Engagement Practices: A Stocktaking Report", www.effectiveinstitutions.org/media/Stocktake_Report_on_Supreme_Audit_Institutions_and_Citizen_Engagement_.pdf.

EUROSAI (2015), *Eurosai Innovations Report*, Vol. 3, Madrid, www.eurosai.org/handle404?exporturi=/export/sites/eurosai/.content/documents/strategic-plan/goal-team-1/10692-001-Eurosai-Innovations-volume-III_final-web-version.pdf (accessed 29 February 2016).

EUROSAI (2014), "Sharing good practices among Supreme Audit Institutions", *EUROSAI Innovations: Volume II*, http://www.eurosai.org/handle404?exporturi=/export/sites/eurosai/.content/documents/strategic-plan/goal-team-1/Innovations-volume-II_Web.pdf.

GAO (Government Accountability Office) (2015), "A Framework for Managing Fraud Risks in Federal Programs", July, www.gao.gov/assets/680/671664.pdf.

Government of Mexico (2016), "Ley de Fiscalización y Rendición de Cuentas de la Federación" [Law on the Accountability and Submission of the Accounts of the Federation], *Diario Oficial de la Federación*, 18 July, www.diputados.gob.mx/LeyesBiblio/pdf/LFRCF.pdf.

Guillan Montero, Aranzazu (2012), "Building bridges: Advancing transparency and participation through the articulation of supreme audit institutions and civil society", paper presented at the 2nd Transatlantic Conference on Transparency Research, Utrecht, 7-9 June (as cited in Effective Institutions Platform, 2014).

Hoque, Zahirul (ed.) (2016), *Making Governments Accountable: The Role of Public Accounts Committees and National Audit Offices*, Routledge, London and New York.

IAACA (International Association of Anti-Corruption Authorities) (n.d.), "Office of the Auditor General", webpage, www.iaaca.org/AntiCorruptionAuthorities/ByCountriesandRegions/S/SouthAfrica1/201202/t20120215_804900.shtml (accessed April 2016).

IAASB (International Auditing and Assurance Standards Board) (2016), "The IAASB's work to explore the growing use of technology in the audit, including data analytics", 21 June, www.iaasb.org/system/files/meetings/files/20160621-IAASB-Agenda_Item_8A-Data-Analytics-Working-Group-Publication-final_0.pdf.

INTOSAI (International Organisation of Supreme Audit Institutions) (2013a), "Fundamental Principles of Compliance Auditing", INTOSAI Harmonisation Project, INTOSAI Professional Standards Committee, Copenhagen, www.issai.org/media/69912/issai-400-english.pdf.

INTOSAI (2013b), "International Standards of Supreme Audit Institutions 12 - The Value and Benefits of Supreme Audit Institutions – Making a Difference in the Lives of Citizens", INTOSAI Professional Standards Committee, Copenhagen, www.intosai.org/issai-executive-summaries/view/article/issai-12-the-value-and-benefits-of-supreme-audit-institutions-making-a-difference-to-the-liv.html.

INTOSAI (2011), "Peer Review Guide", www.pbo-dpb.gc.ca/web/default/files/files/files/Peer_Review_Guide_with_Checklist_EN.pdf. (accessed 9 March 2016).

INTOSAI (2010a), "Quality Control for SAIs", INTOSAI Professional Standards Committee, Copenhagen, www.issai.org/media/12938/issai_40_e_.pdf.

INTOSAI (2010b), "Principles for Transparency and Accountability", INTOSAI Professional Standards Committee, Copenhagen, www.issai.org/media/12930/issai_20_e_.pdf.

INTOSAI (2010c), "Internal Audit Independence in the Public Sector", www.issai.org/media/13349/intosai_gov_9140_e_.pdf.

INTOSAI (1977), "Lima Declaration of Guidelines on Auditing Precepts", *International Standards of Supreme Audit Institutions* (ISSAI), 1, INTOSAI Professional Standard Committee Secretariat, Copenhagen, www.issai.org.

Janssen, R. (2016) *The Art of Audit: Eight Remarkable Government Auditors on Stage*, Amsterdam University Press, The Hague.

NAO (National Audit office) (2012), "Cross government review: Implementing transparency", report by the Comptroller and Auditor General, HC 1833 Session 2010-2012, www.nao.org.uk/wp-content/uploads/2012/04/10121833.pdf.

NAO (n.d.), "Investigations", webpage, www.nao.org.uk/about-us/our-work/investigations/ (accessed April 2016).

The Netherlands Court of Audits (2012), "Quality control", *2011 Annual Report Online*, www.courtofaudit.nl/english/2011_Annual_report/2011_Annual_report:17798/Audits/Quality_control.

New Zealand Controller and Auditor-General (2009), "Annual Report 2008-2009", Office of the Auditor-General, New Zealand, www.oag.govt.nz/2009/2008-09/docs/annual-report.pdf.

NIK (2011), "Ad hoc audits at the request of the Polish Najwyższa Izba Kontroli", www.nik.gov.pl/en/news/ad-hoc-audits-at-the-request-of-the-nik.html (accessed 29 February 2016).

OECD (2016), *Supreme Audit Institutions and Good Governance: Oversight, Insight and Foresight*, OECD Publishing, Paris, http://dx.doi.org/10.1787/9789264263871-en.

OECD (2015), "Recommendation of the Council on Good Budgetary Governance", OECD, www.oecd.org/gov/budgeting/Recommendation-of-the-Council-on-Budgetary-Governance.pdf.

OECD (2014a), "The Principles of Budgetary Governance", July, www.oecd.org/gov/budgeting/Draft-Principles-Budgetary-Governance.pdf.

OECD (2014b), *Chile's Supreme Audit Institution: Enhancing Strategic Agility and Public Trust*, OECD Public Governance Reviews, OECD Publishing, Paris, http://dx.doi.org/10.1787/9789264207561-en.

OECD (2013a), *Brazil's Supreme Audit Institution: The Audit of the Consolidated Year-end Government Report*, OECD Public Governance Reviews, OECD Publishing, Paris, http://dx.doi.org/10.1787/9789264188112-en.

OECD (2013b), "OECD Survey of Benchmark Supreme Audit Institutions", OECD, unpublished.

OECD (2011), *Government at a Glance 2011*, OECD Publishing, Paris, http://dx.doi.org/10.1787/gov_glance-2011-en.

OECD (2010), "Policy Roundtables: Collusion and Corruption in Public Procurement 2010", www.oecd.org/competition/cartels/46235884.pdf.

OECD (2002), "OECD Best Practices for Budget Transparency", *OECD Journal on Budgeting*, Vol. 1/3, http://dx.doi.org/10.1787/budget-v1-art14-en.

Puerto Rico Office of the Comptroller, UK National Audit Office, US Government Accountability (2008) "International Peer Review of the Performance Audit Practice of Mexico's Superior Audit Office", www.intosaicbc.org/mdocs-posts/mexico2008 report/.

SAI India (n.d.), "Big data analytics in SAI India", a presentation by the Comptroller and Auditor General of India, www.google.fr/url?sa=t&rct=j&q=&esrc=s&source=web&cd=2&ved=0ahUKEwjw18C35MfNAhVB1RoKHaNbBmwQFgg7MAE&url=http%3A%2F%2Fportal.tcu.gov.br%2Flumis%2Fportal%2Ffile%2FfileDownload.jsp%3FfileId%3D8A8182A25454C5A8015469F0E2D42BF5&usg=AFQjCNEZ20zwPPjgl2FUq6acxzJx4VfN_A (accessed 18 September 2016).

State Audit Office of Georgia (SAO) (2015), *Twinning SAO-BRH-NIK Newsletter*. Vol. 1, Tbilisi, http://sao.ge/files/auditi/publications/01_Quarterly%20Newsletter_EN.pdf (accessed 29 February 2016).

Supreme Audit Office of Poland (2014), "Peer Review Report on the Supreme Audit Board of the Republic of Indonesia – Badan Pemeriska Keuangan," www.bpk.go.id/assets/files/attachments/attach_page_1399279800.pdf.

TCU (2014), "Open data: A strategy for increased public management transparency and modernization", *Revista do TCU*, September/December 2014, http://revista.tcu.gov.br/ojs/index.php/RTCU/article/viewFile/59/324.

ORGANISATION FOR ECONOMIC CO-OPERATION AND DEVELOPMENT

The OECD is a unique forum where governments work together to address the economic, social and environmental challenges of globalisation. The OECD is also at the forefront of efforts to understand and to help governments respond to new developments and concerns, such as corporate governance, the information economy and the challenges of an ageing population. The Organisation provides a setting where governments can compare policy experiences, seek answers to common problems, identify good practice and work to co-ordinate domestic and international policies.

The OECD member countries are: Australia, Austria, Belgium, Canada, Chile, the Czech Republic, Denmark, Estonia, Finland, France, Germany, Greece, Hungary, Iceland, Ireland, Israel, Italy, Japan, Korea, Latvia, Luxembourg, Mexico, the Netherlands, New Zealand, Norway, Poland, Portugal, the Slovak Republic, Slovenia, Spain, Sweden, Switzerland, Turkey, the United Kingdom and the United States. The European Union takes part in the work of the OECD.

OECD Publishing disseminates widely the results of the Organisation's statistics gathering and research on economic, social and environmental issues, as well as the conventions, guidelines and standards agreed by its members.

OECD PUBLISHING, 2, rue André-Pascal, 75775 PARIS CEDEX 16
(42 2016 30 1 P) ISBN 978-92-64-26473-1 – 2017

www.ingramcontent.com/pod-product-compliance
Lightning Source LLC
Chambersburg PA
CBHW061221240926
51846CB00006B/1299
* 9 7 8 9 2 6 4 2 6 4 7 3 1 *